Crochet for Beginners Relax and Create

Easy Step-by-Step Illustrated Guide to Master Fundamental Stitches while Creating 6 Fun, Affordable Projects that Help Relieve Stress

By

Ella Knotsley

Contents

"In every loop, a world unfolds. With each stitch, a story is spun. Welcome to the gentle art of crochet, where relaxation meets creation, and beginners find solace in the rhythm of the hook."
-Unknown

Introduction

Ey there! Welcome to a journey that will add a splash of creativity, a dash of self-care, and heaps of fun to your life. Crochet isn't just about yarn and hooks; it's about discovering a soothing escape, crafting beautiful pieces, and joining a community as warm and welcoming as the snuggliest blanket you've ever wrapped yourself in. I'm here to guide you through every loop and stitch, making sure that by the end of this book, you'll not only master the basics of crochet but also embrace it as a joyful, therapeutic pastime.

Let's get one thing straight: This book is for everyone. Whether you're 18 or 80, you've never held a crochet hook in your life, or you're picking it up again after a long break, whether right-handed, left-handed, or ambidextrous – this guide is for you. My vision? To create a no-stress, all-fun introduction to crochet that breaks down the basics into bite-sized, easy-to-follow illustrations and instructions. Please think of me as that friend who's always got a tip or two up her sleeve, here to make sure your crochet journey is as smooth and enjoyable as possible.

The chapters cover everything from the simplest chain stitch to cute and quirky projects like bath poufs and temperature blankets. I'll walk you through basic techniques, introduce you to decorative stitches that'll make your projects pop, and even share some advanced tips to keep your hooks flying.

But crochet is more than just a craft; it's a lifeline for many to manage stress and anxiety. The rhythmic motion of the hook, the focus on patterns, and the joy of seeing a project come together can be incredibly calming and meditative. Also, in an increasingly digital and disposable world, crochet offers a sustainable, eco-friendly hobby that reduces waste and adds a personal touch to our surroundings and gifts.

I also want to introduce you to keeping a crochet journal. It's a beautiful way to document your journey, celebrate your progress, and reflect on the patterns and projects that have brought you joy. Plus, it's an excellent tool for revisiting a project or sharing your experiences with the crochet community.

So, whether you're looking to unwind after a long day, create something unique and personal, or learn a new skill, you've come to the right place. I'm beyond excited to get started on this creative journey with you. Remember, every expert crocheter was once a beginner; all it takes is patience, practice, and perseverance. Let's grab our hooks and yarn and let the fun begin!

*** Please scan the QR code to view the projects and images in color ***

Chapter 1

Crafting Magic

THE ARTISTRY OF THE CROCHET HOOK

*** Please scan the QR code to view the projects and images in color ***

I n the realm of crochet, the humble hook holds the key to unlocking a world of creativity. Far from being just a simple tool, the crochet hook is the bridge between yarn and the magic it becomes.

Whether you've picked up a hook in a moment of curiosity at a craft store or received one as a gift, understanding its anatomy is the first step toward turning strands of yarn into treasured creations.

Each part of the hook has been carefully designed to fulfill a specific role, ensuring every loop and stitch is crafted with precision and ease.

1.1 The Anatomy of a Crochet Hook: Understanding Hook Parts and Their Functions

Hook Shaft

The shaft of a crochet hook is comparable to the foundation of a house - it determines the structure and size of every stitch you create. The shaft's length and diameter directly influence the loops' size and, consequently, the tightness or looseness of the fabric you're making. Just as a tailor meticulously selects the thickness of a needle for different fabrics, choosing a hook with the appropriate shaft size is crucial for achieving the desired texture and gauge in crochet projects.

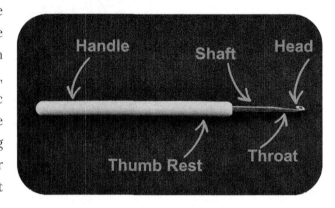

A thicker shaft is typically used for bulkier yarns to create warm, cozy fabrics, ideal for blankets and winter wear. Conversely, a finer shaft pairs well with lightweight yarns, perfect for delicate lace patterns in doilies and summer shawls. This selection process is not just about the end product but also affects the crocheter's comfort during crafting.

Thumb Rest

Consider the sensation of holding a perfectly balanced pen, which feels natural and comfortable in your hand and encourages you to write for hours. The thumb rest on a crochet hook offers a similar comfort for crocheters. Positioned just where your thumb and finger grasp the hook, the thumb rest provides a secure grip, reducing strain on your hand during prolonged crochet sessions. Its design varies among hooks, with some featuring more pronounced rests for those who prefer a tighter grip.

For individuals who crochet for leisure or therapeutic reasons, the significance of the thumb rest cannot be overstated. The subtle difference allows for an afternoon of crocheting without discomfort, making the process as enjoyable as seeing the final creation.

Hook Throat

The throat of a crochet hook plays a pivotal role in creating stitches. Acting as the gateway through which yarn is artfully looped and pulled a smoothly crafted throat ensures the yarn slides effortlessly with each stitch. This part of the hook cradles the yarn, guiding it from the shaft to the point. It is beneficial when working with intricate stitches or slippery yarn.

Imagine trying to thread a needle with frayed thread; the frustration it elicits is similar to working with a hook that catches or splits the yarn. A well-designed throat minimizes these interruptions, making the crochet process more fluid and enjoyable. It's a feature that might not be immediately noticeable to beginners but becomes increasingly appreciated as one's crochet skills advance.

Hook Head

The hook's head is where the true action happens - the part that first interacts with the yarn, diving into stitches to draw them through loops and create the fabric. A finely tuned head is crucial for this task; it must be sharp enough to enter stitches easily but not so sharp as to split the yarn. This delicate balance allows for smooth, efficient crocheting. Working with a hook that has an optimally designed head can be compared to using a chef's knife that's been sharpened to perfection. Just as a sharp blade makes chopping effortless and precise, a well-crafted hook head makes stitching feel like second nature. Whether working through tight stitches of a previous row or navigating the loops of a complex pattern, the hook head design significantly impacts your ability to execute stitches confidently and gracefully. As you become more familiar with the feel of different hooks in your hand, you'll start to appreciate how the nuances in design enhance your crochet journey, making every loop and stitch an expression of your creativity.

1.2 Ergonomics Matter: How to Choose a Crochet Hook That's Comfortable for You

Crocheting is not just about creating; it's also about enjoying the process, stitch by stitch. The right crochet hook can turn hours of crafting into a comfortable and joyful experience. At the same time, the wrong one can lead to frustration and even pain. Understanding the ergonomics of crochet hooks is crucial for your comfort and crafting sessions' longevity. Let's explore how the design of a crochet hook impacts its usability and your comfort.

Grip and Hand Fatigue

Imagine holding a tiny, thin pencil for hours, writing a beautiful story. Soon, your hand cramps, the story's flow is interrupted, and discomfort becomes the main character. Similarly, a crochet hook with a poorly designed grip can lead to hand fatigue, turning your relaxing hobby into a source of strain. Ergonomically designed handles, however, are crafted to fit naturally in the curve of your hand, distributing the pressure evenly and reducing the risk of cramping. These handles often feature a wider diameter and a soft, cushioned material that absorbs some pressure exerted during crocheting, allowing you to crochet for more extended periods without discomfort.

Handle Shape

The shape of the crochet hook's handle is more than just an aesthetic choice; it's about how the tool fits and moves in your hand. Some crocheters prefer a hook with a flatter handle that provides a firm grip and precise control, which is especially useful for intricate patterns and stitches. Others might find a rounded, more bulbous handle fits comfortably in their palm, reducing strain during extended use. Consider how you naturally hold a pen or pencil - this can offer clues to your crocheting style's most comfortable handle shape.

A good practice is to test different handle shapes to see which feels most natural and comfortable for you. Craft stores often have sample hooks available, giving you a feel for how each design impacts your grip and control before purchasing.

Feedback from Crocheters

In the age of information, fellow crocheters' experiences are invaluable resources when selecting the perfect hook. Online forums, social media groups, and product reviews are treasure troves of insights, offering honest feedback on the comfort, durability, and usability of various crochet hooks. Many seasoned crocheters share detailed accounts of how specific hook designs have affected their crafting experience, highlighting both their favorite features and any potential drawbacks.

When sifting through feedback, look for comments from individuals who share similar crocheting habits or preferences. For instance, if you tend to crochet for long stretches, consider reviews mentioning hand fatigue. Or, if you're looking to work with a specific yarn type, look for recommendations tailored to that material. This collective wisdom can guide you toward a crochet hook that fits your hand perfectly and enhances your crocheting experience.

Incorporating these ergonomic considerations into your choice of crochet hook can transform your crafting from a hobby into a comfortable, sustainable practice. The right hook, tailored to your hand's needs and your project's demands, can make each crochet session a joy, allowing your creativity to flow uninterrupted. Remember, the best crochet hook is not necessarily the most expensive or with the most features; it's the one that feels like an extension of your hand, seamlessly facilitating the creation of your crocheted wonders.

Holding the Hook:

Finding the most comfortable way to hold your hook is a personal journey, and what works for one person might not for another.

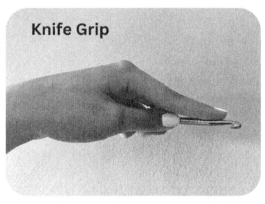

- **The Pencil Grip**: Hold your hook like a pencil, placing your thumb and index finger near the hook's flat part if it has one. This grip offers precision and control, which is ideal for detailed work.

- **The Knife Grip**: Wrap your hand around the hook like a knife. This grip can reduce strain on your wrist and is often preferred for projects requiring more extended periods of crocheting.

1.3 Material World: The Pros and Cons of Different Crochet Hook Materials

When selecting a crochet hook, the material it's made from significantly affects how it feels in your hand, interacts with the yarn, and even the sound it makes as you work. Each material offers a unique set of characteristics that can either enhance or detract from your crocheting experience, depending on your personal preferences and the specifics of the project you're working on.

Aluminum Hooks

Aluminum hooks are popular, especially among beginners, for several reasons. Their smooth surface allows yarn to glide effortlessly, making them ideal for speeding through projects without snagging. They're lightweight yet strong, providing a good balance for those still accustomed to holding the hook and yarn together. However, this smoothness can sometimes be a drawback. For slippery yarns like silk or satin, aluminum hooks might make it challenging to maintain consistent tension, leading to uneven or, in some cases, dropped stitches.

Furthermore, in colder climates or during winter months, aluminum hooks can feel quite cold to the touch, which might be uncomfortable for some crocheters during extended crafting sessions. Conversely, in hot weather or during prolonged use, they can become warm, which some find pleasant and others do not.

Wooden and Bamboo Hooks

For those who prefer a more organic feel, wooden and bamboo hooks provide warmth and a natural grip that many find comfortable and reassuring. Their slightly textured surface offers excellent control over slippery yarns, reducing the chance of stitches sliding off unexpectedly. These hooks are also incredibly lightweight, minimizing hand fatigue during long crocheting sessions.

However, wood and bamboo hooks do have downsides. They're less durable than their metal counterparts, with the potential to snap under too much pressure or wear down over time, especially in smaller sizes. Additionally, the natural grain can vary, leading to slight inconsistencies in smoothness that might catch on delicate yarns.

For those who appreciate the tactile experience of crocheting, the unique characteristics of wooden and bamboo hooks can make each project feel even more unique, similar to how a chef might choose a favorite wooden spoon for certain dishes.

Plastic Hooks

Plastic crochet hooks are an affordable option that offers versatility. They're readily available in larger sizes, especially for those looking to work with bulky or super bulky yarns. Their lightweight nature reduces hand strain, making them suitable for beginners or those with grip issues.

However, the affordability and availability come with trade-offs. Plastic hooks can feel less sturdy, especially in smaller sizes, where the risk of snapping increases. Some crocheters find that plastic hooks lack the smooth glide of aluminum or the warmth of wood, making them feel somewhat flimsy in comparison. Additionally, plastic hooks can become bent or warped over time, mainly when used for tight, demanding projects.

Despite these drawbacks, plastic hooks can be an excellent choice for those exploring the craft or working on large-scale projects where the size of the hook is more critical than the material it's made from.

Specialty Materials

For those looking for something a little different, crochet hooks are also available in a variety of specialty materials, such as glass, carbon fiber, and even resin. These materials often offer unique visual appeal, with beautiful glass hooks that are often hand-blown and feature stunning color combinations.

Carbon fiber hooks combine the lightweight nature of bamboo with the strength of metal, providing a durable option that's comfortable for extended periods. These hooks are typically smooth, with a slight texture that helps grip the yarn without snagging, making them suitable for various projects.

However, these hooks made from specialty materials often come with a higher price tag, which might only be justifiable for some. Additionally, while beautiful, glass hooks can be fragile, requiring careful handling and storage to avoid breakage.

Each material offers a unique crocheting experience, influencing everything from the feel of the hook in your hand to the tension of your stitches. When choosing a crochet hook, consider the project, your comfort, and the overall experience you're looking for. Whether you prefer the smooth glide of aluminum, the warm grip of wood, the affordability of plastic, or the unique appeal of specialty materials, there's a crochet hook perfect for you.

1.4 Size Does Matter: How to Select the Right Hook Size for Your Project

In the nuanced world of crochet, the size of your hook can dramatically affect the outcome of your project. This seemingly simple choice carries weight in the balance between yarn weight compatibility, the nature of your project, personal tension, and the ever-important trial and error process. Let's unwrap these layers to ensure your hook selection sets the stage for success.

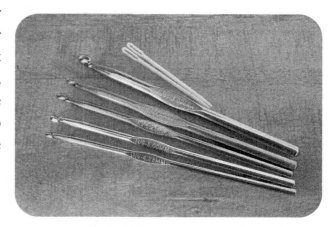

Yarn Weight Compatibility

Yarn comes in a delightful spectrum of weights, each serving a unique purpose and bringing a different texture and density to your projects. From the wispy delicacy of lace weight to the robust chunkiness of super bulky yarn, each type calls for a matching hook size to achieve the desired fabric. This pairing is not random, but a harmonious match that ensures the hook correctly supports each stitch, allowing for even tension and definition.

- Lace weight yarns, being the thinnest, pair well with hooks in the 2.25 mm (B) to 3.5 mm (E) range, ideal for delicate shawls and intricate doilies.

- Light to medium-weight yarns, including sport and worsted, often call for hooks from 3.5 mm (E) to 5.5 mm (I), making them versatile for various projects, from garments to soft toys.

- Bulky and super bulky yarns revel in the larger hook sizes of 6 mm (J) and above, lending themselves to quick projects with a cozy, chunky finish, like blankets and scarves.

Selecting the hook size that aligns with your yarn weight ensures the stitches are neither too tight and stiff nor too loose and holey, striking the perfect balance for your project.

CROCHET HOOK CONVERSIONS		
US	METRIC	UK/CANADA
B/1	2.25mm	13
C/2	2.75mm	12
-	3mm	10
D/3	3.25mm	-
E/4	3.5mm	9
F/5	3.75	-
G/6	4mm	8
7	4.5mm	7
H/8	5mm	6
I/9	5.5mm	5
J/10	6mm	4
K/10.5	6.5mm	3
-	7mm	2
L/11	8mm	0
M/13	9mm	00
N/15	10mm	000
P/16	12mm	-
S	20mm	-

Personal Tension

How you hold your yarn and hook, combined with the force you apply while crafting, creates your unique tension. Some crocheters have a tighter tension, pulling stitches closer together. In contrast, others work more loosely, giving their fabric a lighter, airier feel. Recognizing your tension style is crucial as it might lead you to adjust the hook size to achieve the gauge specified in a pattern.

- If your tension is tight, going up a hook size allows you to meet the pattern's gauge without altering your natural crocheting rhythm.

- Conversely, if your tension is loose, a smaller hook can help tighten up those stitches, aligning your work with the pattern's expectations.

- Holding the Yarn: Experiment with draping the yarn over your index finger, under your middle finger, and then over your ring finger, adjusting the wrap until you find the tension that gives you even stitches and comfortable flow. Some crocheters thread the yarn through a ring on their index finger to maintain consistent tension.

Navigating the selection of the right crochet hook size reveals that this choice is far from arbitrary. It's a considered decision that influences your project's success, the crafting process's pleasure, and the development of your skills as a crochet artist. Paying due attention to yarn weight compatibility, project type considerations, and personal tension and embracing trial and error allows you to create a fulfilling crochet experience that yields beautiful, cherished creations.

1.5 Right-handed vs. Left-handed Hooks: Myths and Facts

In the tapestry of crochet, the distinction between right-handed and left-handed hooks weaves a narrative filled with myths and realities. Untangling these threads is pivotal for newcomers and seasoned crocheters, ensuring that the craft is accessible and enjoyable for everyone, regardless of which hand they favor.

Ergonomic Differences

The crochet hooks' landscape offers various ergonomic designs tailored to enhance comfort and reduce strain during those long, immersive crafting sessions. Given the majority demographic, it's a common belief that these ergonomic features are specific to right-handed individuals. However, the truth is more inclusive. Many ergonomic hooks are designed to be ambidextrous, catering to the comfort of both right and left-handed crocheters. The key lies not in the orientation of the hook but in the design of the handle, which should conform naturally to the contours of the hand, allowing for a relaxed grip that prevents fatigue.

Finding an ergonomic hook that feels right for left-handed crocheters might require some trial. The subtle differences in grip and hand movement mean that what works for a right-handed individual might provide a different level of comfort for someone who crochets with their left hand. Paying attention to how the hook feels in your hand, how easily it allows you to maintain your grip without exerting too much pressure, and whether it facilitates a smooth crocheting rhythm are all crucial factors in selecting the perfect ergonomic hook.

Adaptability

Left-handed crocheters often adapt to a world of crafts designed with right-handed individuals in mind. This adaptability becomes a strength, especially in crochet, where technique and comfort are paramount. Many left-handed crocheters excel using the same hooks as their right-handed peers, developing a crocheting style that's both effective and uniquely theirs.

This adaptability extends to following patterns and tutorials, predominantly written from a right-handed perspective. With time and practice, left-handed crocheters learn to invert these instructions, viewing them through a mirror and applying them to their left-handed technique. Once honed, this skill allows for a seamless transition between patterns and projects, making the crochet world accessible regardless of hand dominance.

Specialty Hooks

While the functional difference between right-handed and left-handed crocheters is minimal, the market does offer "left-handed" hooks. These are often less about the hook itself and more about the ergonomics of the handle. For some left-handed individuals, these specialty hooks might provide extra comfort, fitting more naturally into their grip and facilitating smoother crocheting movements.

It's important to note that these specialty hooks are unnecessary for left-handed crocheting. They are an option, one of many in the diverse toolkit available to crocheters. Exploring these options, from standard hooks to those with specialized ergonomic designs, allows each crocheter to find the tools that best suit their needs, preferences, and crocheting style.

Ultimately, the choice of crochet hook - whether standard or ergonomic, marketed for right-handed or left-handed use - is deeply personal. It's about finding the tool that feels like an extension of your hand, one that effortlessly translates your creative vision into the stitches and patterns that make up your crocheting projects.

Chapter 2

The Heart of Crochet

Yarn Unraveled

Picture this: a cozy evening, your favorite spot by the window, a warm cup of tea by your side, and in your hands, the soft, comforting feel of yarn gliding through your fingers as you crochet. The yarn isn't just a thread; it's the soul of your project, infusing character, warmth, and texture into every stitch.

Natural vs. Synthetic

- Natural Fibers: They're like the fresh produce of the yarn world. Wool, cotton, silk, and bamboo fall into this category, each bringing its unique touch. Wool is renowned for its warmth and elasticity, making it a go-to for cozy winter projects. Conversely, cotton is your summer yarn - breathable, soft, and perfect for lighter creations. Silk adds a luxurious sheen and drape, ideal for sophisticated garments. At the same time, bamboo yarn is eco-friendly, with a lovely luster and antibacterial properties..

- Synthetic Fibers: These convenience foods of yarn - acrylic, polyester, and nylon are the leading players. They're durable, easy to care for, and resist shrinking or felting, making them a practical choice for everyday items. Their color range is like a rainbow on steroids, offering vibrant hues that don't fade quickly.

The choice between natural and synthetic fibers often depends on the project, your preference, and sometimes your budget. While natural yarns can offer a more luxurious feel and better breathability, synthetic yarns are unbeatable for their durability and colorfastness

Blended Yarns

Sometimes, two heads (or, in this case, fibers) are better than one. Blended yarns mix fibers to marry their best qualities:

- Warmth and Durability: Wool-acrylic blends offer the warmth of wool with the durability and easy care of acrylic.

- Softness and Strength: Cotton-silk blends combine cotton's softness with silk's strength and sheen, resulting in a luxurious yarn that's sturdy and gentle against the skin.

- Elasticity and Cost-Effectiveness: Blending an expensive fiber like cashmere with a more affordable one like polyester can produce a yarn that's both luxurious and accessible.

The downside? Sometimes, blends can dilute the very qualities you sought in the first place. A wool-acrylic blend, for instance, might not be as warm as pure wool or as durable as 100% acrylic. It's all about finding the right balance for your project and preferences.

2.1 Weighty Decisions: How Yarn Weight Influences Crochet Projects

Navigating through the myriad of yarn choices for your next crochet project, you'll quickly find that the weight of the yarn plays a pivotal role in the outcome of your creative endeavors. The yarn weight system is a beacon, guiding the path to selecting the perfect yarn for your project. This system categorizes yarns from lace to jumbo, each designed with specific projects in mind. Understanding this classification unlocks a world where each stitch contributes to the fabric in a precise manner.

Stitch Definition

The yarn weight greatly influences the clarity with which each stitch presents itself in your finished project. Lighter weights, such as fingering or sport, offer a canvas where stitches can shine individually, making them ideal for projects requiring fine details. These yarns allow complex stitch patterns to stand out, perfect for heirloom quality lacework or garments where every stitch tells a story.

Worsted and bulky weights give stitches a bolder presence, creating fabrics that feel substantial. These yarns excel in projects where you want the texture to take the lead, like ribbed hats or chunky scarves.

Project Suitability

The union of project and yarn weight is comparable to choosing the right instrument for a music piece; the harmony created is undeniable. Lighter weights lend themselves to garments and delicate accessories, where drape and detail are paramount. Imagine a summer top crafted from a fine cotton blend yarn, its fabric flowing and breathable, adorned with subtle stitch patterns that catch the eye.

Heavyweights are your allies for home decor and winter wear. They transform into plush throws that invite cozy evenings by the fire or warm sweaters that fend off the chilliest days. These yarns work up quickly, making them perfect candidates for projects you want to enjoy or gift without delay.

Gauge and Swatching

The most critical role of yarn weight in project planning is achieving the correct gauge. Gauge measures how many stitches and rows fit into a given inch or centimeter, a crucial factor in determining the size and fit of the finished project. Here, swatching becomes an indispensable step that seasoned crocheters know to take advantage of.

Creating a swatch, a small sample piece, using the yarn and hook intended for the project, offers a sneak peek into how the finished fabric will look and feel. It's a practical way to ensure that the yarn weight, combined with your personal crochet style, meets the pattern's requirements. If your swatch is too small or too large compared to the pattern gauge, adjusting your hook size can bring you back on track, saving you from potential disappointment later. To check your gauge, crochet a small sample square using the stitch specified in the pattern. Measure the width and height within a 4-inch square. If your gauge matches the pattern, great! If not, you may need to adjust your hook size or tension.

Swatching also presents an opportunity to see how the yarn behaves after washing and blocking, mirroring the care it will receive throughout its life. Some yarns bloom, softening and expanding, while others might shrink or change texture. This knowledge allows you to make informed decisions, ensuring the durability and enjoyment of your crochet projects.

2.2 Color Theory in Crochet: Choosing Colors for Your Project

The moment you decide on the colors for your crochet project is magical. It's when your creation starts to take on a life of its own, whispering stories of mood, atmosphere, and personality. The colors you choose breathe life into your stitches, transforming them into a tapestry rich with emotion and expression. Understanding color theory can elevate your projects from beautiful to breathtaking.

Color Harmony

At its core, color harmony involves combining colors in a way that is pleasing to the eye. It's about creating a balance that evokes a sense of order and aesthetics. There are several methods to achieve this balance:

- Complementary Colors: These are colors opposite each other on the color wheel, like blue and orange. They create a vibrant look, perfect for projects that aim to stand out.

- Analogous Colors: These colors sit side by side on the color wheel, such as green, blue-green, and blue. They offer a serene and comfortable design, ideal for projects aiming for a subtle or calming effect.

- Triadic Colors: This scheme involves colors evenly spaced around the color wheel, such as red, yellow, and blue. It brings a lively presence to projects, packed with a harmonious contrast.

Experimenting with these combinations can open up a world of possibilities, turning each project into an exploration of color and its impact on our perceptions and emotions.

Mood and Theme

Colors can convey mood and emphasize the theme of your crochet project. Warm colors like red, orange, and yellow can evoke warmth, passion, or excitement, making them perfect for energetic and lively creations. On the other hand, cool colors such as blue, green, and purple tend to have a calming effect, ideal for projects meant to soothe or relax.

When planning your project, think about the story you want to tell. Is it a cheerful baby blanket, a cozy autumn shawl, or a sophisticated purse? Let the colors you choose narrate the story, enhancing the emotional connection between the creation and its recipient.

Variegated Yarns

Variegated yarns, with their mesmerizing shifts in color, offer a unique avenue for creativity. These yarns can range from subtle gradients to bold, contrasting color changes, providing an effortless way to introduce multiple colors into a project without changing yarns. However, they also present unique challenges, such as:

- Color Pooling: Sometimes, colors in a variegated yarn may cluster or "pool" in certain areas, creating unexpected patterns. While some find this effect delightful, others prefer a more uniform distribution of color. Manipulating stitch counts, hook size, or even how you hold the yarn can help manage pooling, turning a potential challenge into an opportunity for creativity.

- Balancing Act: Consider how the colors interact in projects using variegated and solid-colored yarns. A solid color can help offset the busyness of a variegated yarn, providing "breathing space" for the eyes and highlighting the yarn's beauty.

Working with variegated yarns is like painting with a palette where the colors blend seamlessly. It invites you to play, experiment, and sometimes, let the yarn take the lead in the dance of creation.

Color Fastness

Imagine the heartbreak of finishing a vibrant, multicolored project, only to have the colors bleed and muddy during its first wash. Colorfastness refers to a yarn's ability to retain color without bleeding or fading over time. It's an especially crucial consideration for projects that will be washed frequently or exposed to sunlight.

To ensure your projects retain their intended beauty:

- Test Before You Crochet: Before starting your project, test the yarn's color fastness by soaking a small piece in warm water. If the water turns color, consider setting the dye using a fixative or choosing a different yarn for projects requiring durability.

- Wash With Care: Following the yarn label's instructions can significantly reduce the risk of color bleeding. Cold water and gentle detergents are often your best allies in preserving the colors of your crochet items.

Choosing colors for your crochet project is an adventure, a journey through hues and shades that can transform the most straightforward pattern into a masterpiece. It's more than just aesthetics; it's about evoking feelings, telling stories, and bringing your creative vision to life.

2.3 Reading Yarn Labels: What You Need to Know Before You Buy

The excitement can be palpable when you're standing in the aisle of your local craft store or browsing online, surrounded by skeins of yarn in every hue imaginable. But before you fill your basket, there's a secret language you'll want to crack: the yarn label. This little band wrapped around each skein is a treasure trove of information that can make or break your next project. Let's peel back the layers of the yarn label to reveal the key details you need to pay attention to.

Yarn Weight and Category

First, yarn weight isn't about how heavy a skein is but rather the thickness of the yarn strand. The Craft Yarn Council has standardized this into categories, ranging from 0 (lace) to 7 (jumbo). Each category has a symbol, often a skein with a number inside, and this is your first clue in matching yarn to the project. For example, if your heart is set on a delicate shawl, a yarn marked with a '2' (fine) might be your best bet. While for a cozy blanket, those marked with '5' (bulky) or '6' (super bulky) will speed up the process and add that plush feel.

- Lace (0): Perfect for light shawls and intricate details.

- Super Fine (1): Ideal for socks and lightweight garments.

- Fine (2): Works well for baby items and light sweaters.

- Light (3): A versatile choice for various projects, including toys and garments.

- Medium (4): Great for blankets, hats, and scarves.

- Bulky (5) and Super Bulky (6) are the go-to's for quick projects or those needing a thick, warm finish.

- Jumbo (7): Used for arm knitting or aiming for a super chunky texture.

Care Instructions

Imagine spending hours on a beautiful crochet blanket only to have it shrink in the wash. To avoid such heartbreak, the care symbols on the yarn label are your best friends. These icons indicate whether the yarn is machine washable, the recommended water temperature, whether it can be tumble dried, and how to safely iron or dry clean your creation. Adhering to these guidelines ensures your hard work remains as beautiful as the day you finish it.

- Machine Washable Symbol: A washtub icon is safe for the machine, often accompanied by a maximum temperature.

- Tumble Dry: A square with a circle inside indicates tumble drying is okay, sometimes with a dot inside to denote temperature.

- Ironing: An iron symbol, often crossed out for yarns that don't tolerate heat well.

- Dry Clean: A circle, usually with a letter inside, guiding you to the correct dry cleaning method, if applicable.

Dye Lot Numbers

The dye lot number is crucial for projects requiring more than one skein of yarn. This number ensures that all skeins come from the same dye batch, offering color uniformity across your project. Slight variations can occur between batches, so skeins with the same dye lot number keep your work looking cohesive. Suppose the label mentions 'No Dye Lot.' In that case, the manufacturer guarantees color consistency across batches, giving you more flexibility.

- Consistent Color: Matching dye lot numbers is critical to avoiding noticeable color shifts in larger projects.

- Planning: Buy enough yarn from the same dye lot at the outset to avoid running out mid-project.

Chapter 3

The Left-Handed Crocheter's Guide to Harmony

I magine picking up a hook that was made just for you. It's not about the material it's made of or its color. It's about how it fits into your left hand as if it's an extension of your thoughts, turning yarn into fabric as smoothly as words flow into a conversation. This chapter is dedicated to all the left-handed crocheters navigating a predominantly right-handed world of loops and stitches. You're not just making do; you're adapting and thriving, creating beautiful pieces with a hook in the left hand.

3.1 Mirror Techniques: Adapting Right-Handed Instructions for Lefties

Visual Reversal

Crochet patterns are vast, but most are written with right-handed crafters in mind. The art of visual reversal is the key to unlocking this treasure trove for left-handed crocheters. It's like reading a book in front of a mirror; the words are the same, but you approach them from a different angle. When you come across a right-handed diagram, imagine flipping it horizontally. This mental flip helps you understand where to insert your hook and in which direction to work, ensuring your project develops correctly.

Real-life example: If a pattern instructs you to increase on the right side for a right-handed crocheter, you, as a left-handed artist, would increase on the left. It's a simple switch that makes all the difference.

Using Mirrors

A physical mirror can be a surprisingly effective tool for understanding right-handed diagrams. Place the diagram next to a mirror and follow the reflection. This technique provides a left-handed view of each step, making it easier to grasp how each stitch is formed and where to place your hook next. It's like learning a dance step by mirroring the instructor's moves - suddenly, everything clicks into place.

Finding Left-Handed Tutorials

Thankfully, the digital world is full of resources tailored for left-handed crocheters. From YouTube tutorials to dedicated blog posts, a wealth of information is just a click away. These resources often provide step-by-step visuals or videos that show how to hold the yarn and hook, make stitches, and read patterns from a left-handed perspective. It's like having a personal crochet instructor by your side, guiding you through each step.

3.2 Left-Handed Resources: Finding Patterns and Tutorials

Navigating the crochet world as a left-hander can sometimes feel like decoding a complex puzzle. However, the pieces fit together more smoothly with the right resources at your fingertips. Whether diving into forums that buzz with fellow left-handed crocheters or discovering books that demystify left-handed techniques, a wealth of knowledge is waiting to be tapped into.

Community Support

The sense of belonging to a community that understands your needs can be incredibly uplifting. Online forums and social media groups are bustling hubs where left-handed crocheters gather to exchange tips, share triumphs, and, sometimes, voice their frustrations. These platforms offer more than just advice; they provide a sense of camaraderie. Here, you can find:

- Facebook groups are dedicated to left-handed crochet. Members post tutorials, answer each other's queries and celebrate completed projects.

- Forums on Ravelry specifically for left-handers, offering a space to discuss pattern modifications and techniques.

- Left-handed crafters use Instagram hashtags to showcase their work, providing a visual feast of inspiration and a way to connect with like-minded individuals.

Left-Handed Pattern Adjustments

While most patterns cater to right-handed crocheters, adapting them for left-hand use is more straightforward than it might seem. The trick lies in understanding the pattern's structure and then mirroring it. Here are a few pointers:

- You'll work oppositely on motifs that lean or spiral in a specific direction to achieve the same effect.

- Remember, the foundation chain doesn't change; it's the direction of your work that does.

Sharing these adaptations within your craft circles or online forums helps you. It paves the way for future left-handers who might encounter the same challenges.

Books and Videos

While the internet is a goldmine of tutorials and guides, there's something special about having a tangible book or a go-to video channel that speaks directly to left-handers. Consider adding these to your resource library:

- "Crochet for Lefties" by Donna Wolfe is a book that breaks down basics to advanced stitches with clear illustrations and step-by-step instructions for the left-handed crocheter.

- The Crochet Crowd's YouTube channel, which includes videos focused on left-handed techniques, offers visual learners a clear view of how stitches are formed and worked.

- "Left-Handed Crochet" by Regina Hurlburt explores not just the how-tos but also delves into troubleshooting common issues left-handers might face.

Each resource is designed to make the learning curve less steep, transforming challenges into enjoyable milestones in your crochet adventure. Tapping into these resources can significantly enrich your crocheting experience, opening up a world where left-handers are accommodated and celebrated.

3.3 Common Challenges for Left-Handed Crocheters and How to Overcome Them

Navigating the crochet world as a left-hander can sometimes feel like trying to decode an ancient script meant for right-handers. But fear not! With a few tweaks and a dash of creativity, those seemingly impossible challenges transform into stepping stones toward your mastery of crochet. Let's explore some common hurdles and how to leap over them quickly.

Stitch Direction

Creating a piece that looks uniform and follows the intended pattern direction can sometimes trip up left-handed crocheters. When crocheting from left to right, instead of the more conventional right to left, paying attention to the orientation of your stitches is crucial. This ensures your work looks different from a mirror image of what you intended, especially when working on projects with a definite direction, such as letters or asymmetrical designs.

- Flip the Script: For patterns that rely heavily on symmetry, imagine working backward from the last step or flipping the visual pattern as if looking through a mirror. This mental flip helps maintain the directionality of stitches, keeping the integrity of the design intact.

- Mark Your Starting Point: Stitch markers or a small piece of yarn in a contrasting color can help you identify the beginning of your rounds or rows. This visual cue becomes your north star, guiding each stitch to follow the correct path around your work.

Reading Patterns and Diagrams

Patterns and diagrams are like treasure maps leading to the finished piece. However, for left-handers, these maps are often drawn in a language that feels foreign. Here's how you can decipher them:

- Reorient the Diagrams: Visualize the diagrams as if they're flipped horizontally. This might mean taking a physical copy and holding it to a light source backward or using photo editing software to flip the image.

- Translate the Instructions: Mentally replacing "left" with "right" and vice versa in written instructions can make a world of difference. It's a simple switch that aligns the pattern with your natural working direction.

- Create Your Own Annotations: Be bold and write on your patterns or diagrams. Mark them with notes that make sense, highlighting any changes you need to remember as you work.

Crocheting as a left-hander brings its own set of puzzles to solve. Still, with these strategies, you'll find yourself weaving through projects with the same ease and joy as any right-hander. The key lies in adapting the world of crochet to fit your unique perspective, turning what might seem like obstacles into opportunities for growth and creativity.

3.4 Leftie Pride: Embracing Your Unique Crochet Style

In a world where most tools and techniques are designed for right-handed individuals, being a left-handed crocheter is akin to being a rare gem. It's not merely about how you hold your hook or yarn; it's about the distinct perspective you bring to the craft. Your unique approach enriches the tapestry of crochet, adding depth and diversity.

Unique Advantages

Left-handed crocheters possess advantages that set them apart. Imagine the beauty of symmetry in projects, where your left-handed creations complement those made by right-handers, offering a mirror image that's both striking and harmonious. Your ability to see patterns and projects from a different angle challenges the norm. It pushes the boundaries of creativity, leading to innovative designs and techniques. Moreover, your adaptability, honed from navigating a right-handed world, makes you skilled at troubleshooting and customizing, transforming obstacles into opportunities for growth.

As we wrap up this exploration of what it means to be a left-handed crocheter, it's clear that your role in the tapestry of this craft is invaluable. Your unique approach challenges traditional methods and enriches the crochet world, making it a more vibrant space.

Chapter 4

The Language of Crochet

*** Please scan the QR code to view the projects and images in color ***

Imagine flipping through an old, well-loved cookbook. The pages are worn and stained from years of use, each marking a story of meals past. But among the familiar recipes, you stumble upon a notation that seems like a secret code, shorthand known only to the author. Diving into crochet patterns for the first time can feel like interpreting a secret language full of abbreviations and symbols that, at first glance, might as well be hieroglyphics. But fear not, for just as with that cookbook, once you crack the code, a world of creativity opens up before you.

The beauty of crochet is its ability to convey so much with so little. A few simple abbreviations on a page blossom into intricate patterns and textures under your fingers. This chapter is your Rosetta Stone, a guide to unlocking the meaning behind these crochet abbreviations and shorthand symbols, enabling you to bring the patterns they describe to life.

Decoding Crochet Abbreviations: A Comprehensive Guide

Here's a starter list of the most common abbreviations you'll encounter and what they stand for:

- ch: chain

- sc: single crochet

- dc: double crochet

- hdc: half double crochet

- sl st: slip stitch

- st(s): stitch(es)

- yo: yarn over

- yoh: yarn over hook

- rep = repeat

Understanding these abbreviations is your first step in following patterns and bringing your crochet projects to life. Remember, every crocheter was once where you are now. Practice and patience are your best friends here.

Abbreviation Variations: Understanding that some patterns may use different abbreviations, especially from other countries.

Crochet is a language spoken worldwide, and dialects exist just like any language. For instance, what's called single crochet (sc) in the U.S. is known as double crochet (dc) in the U.K. Here are a few tips to navigate these variations:

- Check the pattern source: Look for clues about the pattern's origin. Often, the terminology used will align with the country of publication.

- Look for a glossary: Some patterns include a list of abbreviations used, along with their definitions. This can be a handy reference if you come across unfamiliar terms.

- When in doubt, Google it: Many online resources explain the differences between U.S. and U.K. crochet terms.

Creating Your Own Abbreviation Cheat Sheet

As you grow more comfortable with crochet patterns, certain abbreviations and instructions become second nature. But in the beginning, having a quick reference can be invaluable. Why not create your own abbreviation cheat sheet? Here's how:

- Start with the basics: Jot down the most common abbreviations and their meanings. Include U.S. and U.K. terms if you're using patterns from various sources.

- Add as you go: When you encounter a new abbreviation, add it to your list. This way, your cheat sheet grows with your skills.

- Keep it handy: Store your cheat sheet with your crochet supplies. Having it within easy reach means you can quickly consult it whenever needed.

This personalized guide not only aids in your current projects but also records your learning journey. Reflecting on your learning and seeing how far you've come is extremely satisfying.

4.1 Anatomy of a Crochet Pattern: Breaking Down the Basics

When you're holding a crochet pattern for the first time, it's like standing at the entrance of a maze. You know there's a path through, but figuring out where to start can be overwhelming. Patterns are the maps of the crochet world, guiding us stitch by stitch to our final creation. They have their own structure, a kind of platform that, once understood, makes navigating much simpler.

Pattern Structure

Every crochet pattern typically starts with a header. This is where you find the project title, a photo or sketch of the finished item, and sometimes a difficulty rating.

Next comes the materials list. Here, yarn type, color, and quantity are specified, along with the hook size and any additional tools or notions you'll need. It's your shopping list, ensuring you have everything on hand before you begin.

The instructions follow, often starting with a gauge swatch recommendation. This section is the heart of the pattern, where each step is outlined, usually in order of execution. It's your step-by-step guide through the maze.

Some patterns include finishing instructions detailing assembling pieces, weaving in ends, or adding embellishments. This section ensures your project looks polished and complete.

Symbol Interpretation

Crochet patterns often use symbols to convey instructions more efficiently. Think of them as shorthand or emojis in text messages - they pack a lot of information into a small space.

Asterisks:

- (*) One asterisk: Repeat the instructions following the asterisk as directed. It's like hitting the replay button until you reach a specified point.

- (**) Two asterisks: Repeat instructions between asterisks as many times as directed or repeat at specific locations.

Parentheses ( ) work instructions within parentheses as many times as directed or group stitches that are worked into a single stitch or space. Imagine gathering a bunch of flowers into one hand - that's what you're doing with your stitches.

Brackets [ ] are often used inside a line of instructions to highlight a series of stitches repeated several times across a row. Work instructions in brackets as many times as directed. It's like copying and pasting a sentence into a document.

Getting comfortable with these symbols can streamline your crochet process, making it easier to follow complex patterns.

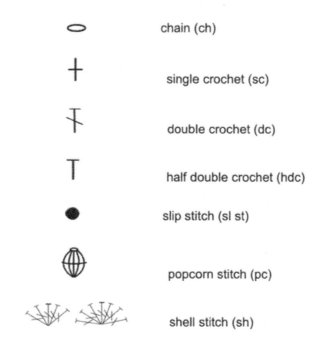

CROCHET STITCH SYMBOLS

chain (ch)

single crochet (sc)

double crochet (dc)

half double crochet (hdc)

slip stitch (sl st)

popcorn stitch (pc)

shell stitch (sh)

Project Planning

Before diving hook-first into a project, some planning can save you time and yarn. Here's a checklist to guide you:

- Please read through the pattern: It sounds simple, but it is like reading a recipe before cooking. You'll understand the steps involved and any potential tricky spots.

- Gather your materials: Ensure you have all the yarn and tools specified. It's frustrating to pause your work because you're missing something essential.

- Make a gauge swatch: This step cannot be overstated, but it is not always required for every project. A gauge swatch is your project's fitting room, ensuring everything will size up correctly.

- How to make a gauge swatch: Look at the pattern to see if it specifies the gauge. Some patterns provide step-by-step instructions for a gauge swatch, while others name a stitch that you'll crochet into a 4" x 4" swatch.

- Mark your pattern: Use a highlighter or sticky notes to mark key instructions or areas of focus. It's like leaving breadcrumbs for yourself to follow.

- Set milestones: Break the project into smaller, manageable sections. Reaching these mini-goals is rewarding and keeps your motivation high.

Approaching a crochet pattern with this foundation of understanding transforms it from a daunting code to a trusted guide.

4.2 From Diagrams to Projects: How to Read Crochet Charts

Crochet charts, or diagrams, can seem like a maze of dots, lines, and symbols at first glance. However, they hold the key to visualizing patterns in a way that words alone sometimes cannot. These charts offer a bird's-eye view of a project, showcasing how each stitch connects and builds upon the next. For those who find traditional written instructions challenging or visual learners eager to see how their project will come together, learning to read these charts can be a game-changer.

Chart Basics

At the heart of understanding crochet charts is getting to know the symbols. Each symbol represents a specific crochet stitch or technique, from simple chain stitches to more complex trebles and bobbles. The beauty of these symbols is their universality; once you learn them, you can understand crochet patterns from anywhere in the world, regardless of the language in which the instructions are written.

Charts are read differently depending on whether you crochet right-handed or left-handed. Right-handers typically read charts from right to left on odd-numbered rows and left to right on even-numbered rows, mimicking how the fabric is created. Left-handers do the opposite. A solid circle might represent a single crochet, while an 'X' could represent a double crochet. Chains are often depicted as ovals or small circles, leading you like breadcrumbs to the next stitch.

Comparing Written Patterns to Charts

Marrying written instructions with their charted counterparts can illuminate the path of a pattern, turning tricky passages into straightforward roads. Here's how they complement each other:

- Written patterns provide the details - how many stitches to chain, where to join a round, or when to change colors. Charts offer a snapshot, a visual cue that helps you anticipate the shape and flow of your project.

- When the wording feels dense or the sequence of stitches complex, referring to the chart can often clarify the intended outcome. You see the stitches as they should appear, providing an instant check against your work.

- Using both allows you to double-check your understanding. Suppose the written instructions say to repeat a sequence across the row, and the chart shows this repetition visually. In that case, you're more likely to grasp and execute the concept correctly.

Embarking on the journey to read crochet charts equips you with a valuable skill that enhances your crochet experience. It bridges the gap between envisioning and bringing a project to life, offering a clear map to follow and the tools to navigate it successfully.

4.3 Tips for Troubleshooting Common Pattern Problems

With its intricate stitches and patterns, crochet can sometimes lead you into a tangled mess of yarn. It's all part of the process. There will be moments when the pattern in front of you might as well be in ancient script, and errors sneak into your work like uninvited guests. However, there's always a way to untangle the knots and continue crafting something beautiful.

Misinterpreting Instructions

Sometimes, how we interpret a pattern's instructions can lead us off course. It's common to glance too quickly and miss a crucial detail or need clarification on what's being asked. Here are a few ways to avoid these pitfalls:

- Take your time reading through the instructions before you start. A thorough initial read can prevent many errors.

- Look up any unclear terms or abbreviations. Even if you think you know them, a quick check can prevent mistakes later.

- If a section of the pattern seems confusing, try finding a video tutorial or step-by-step guide for that specific technique. Sometimes, seeing it in action makes all the difference.

Correcting Errors Mid-Project

Discovering a mistake several rows back in your work is disheartening, but it's not the end of the world. Before you consider unraveling hours of work, here are a few strategies to fix errors without starting over:

- If the mistake is a missed stitch and you've only gone a few rows past it, you can use a crochet hook to "pull" the correct stitch up through the rows. This technique benefits simple missed stitches but might only work for some complex patterns.

- For errors that involve adding or skipping stitches, causing the project to veer off the intended shape, consider whether you can adjust future rows to compensate without significantly affecting the final product.

- When you realize a pattern repeat is off, see if you can creatively adapt the design. Sometimes, what starts as an error can lead to a unique, personalized touch.

Asking for Help

There's a vast community of crocheters out there, from local clubs to online forums, and most are more than happy to lend their expertise:

- Local yarn shops often have knowledgeable staff who can advise or direct you to resources that can help

- Online crochet forums and social media groups are treasure troves of information. Don't be shy about posting a photo of your work and asking for advice; crocheters are a friendly bunch!

- Look for a crochet buddy or mentor. Having someone to crochet with and ask real-time questions can be incredibly helpful.

Navigating the intricacies of crochet patterns is a skill honed over time. With every stitch and every project, you'll find your confidence growing. Mistakes and misinterpretations become less daunting, not just hurdles to overcome but opportunities to learn and innovate. Each challenge faced and solved adds another layer to your crochet journey, enriching your experience and broadening your skills.

Chapter 5

Basic Crochet Stitches and Techniques

Crochet hooks are like keys to a secret garden where creativity blooms in every corner. Just as a gardener nurtures seeds into blossoms, a crocheter transforms yarn into art. Every masterpiece starts with a single loop, a humble beginning from which beauty grows. This chapter guides you to the stitches that form the foundation of all crochet projects, beginning with the most fundamental: the chain stitch.

5.1 The Mighty Chain Stitch: The Foundation of All Crochet Projects

Foundation of Crochet

The chain stitch is the cornerstone upon which crochet is built. Think of it as the first row of bricks in a wall or the initial sketch lines of a drawing. It sets the stage for determining the length and foundation of your project, be it a cozy blanket or a delicate shawl. The rest of the project can find footing with a stable, well-crafted chain. This stitch turns a length of yarn into a base for creation, ready to be built upon with more complex stitches.

Creating a Slip Knot

Every chain stitch (ch) begins with a slip knot. You cannot start a crochet project without a slip knot. This is your anchor, the point where yarn and hook first meet.

Slip Knot

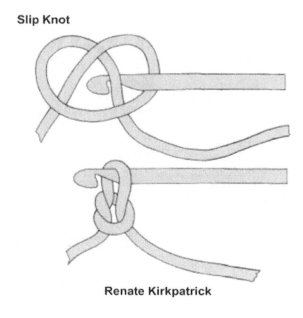

Renate Kirkpatrick

Slip Knot Directions:

1. Start with 7-8 inches of yarn.

2. Take the tail end of the yarn and drape it over the working end of the yarn to form a loop.

3. Fold the tail end of the yarn under the loop, forming a pretzel.

4. Pick up your hook and insert it through the first loop of the pretzel.

5. While holding both ends of the yarn, pull up the hook to make your slip knot.

Note: Pulling on the tail end of your yarn will tighten the loop, while pulling on the working end will loosen it.

Step-by-Step Chain Stitch Instructions

Materials:

- Yarn of choice (cotton worsted weight #4 (medium) - very popular)

- Crochet hook suitable for your yarn (H-8/5mm - very popular size)

- Scissors

Abbreviations Used:

ch = chain

yo = yarn over

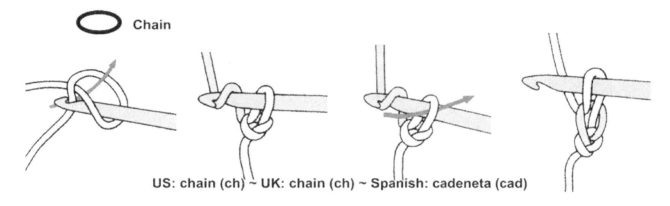

Special thanks to Renate Kirkpatrick for the beautiful stitch illustrations - Ren's Fibre Art
https://rensfibreart.wordpress.com/handy-crochet-tips-tricks-2/stitch-overview/

1. Hold the crochet hook in your dominant hand. You can use the pencil grip (like holding a pencil) or the knife grip (like holding a knife).

2. With your other hand, hold the tail end of the slip knot. This will help you maintain tension on the yarn.

3. Yarn Over (yo):

- Wrap the working yarn (the yarn attached to the ball) over the hook from back to front (called a "yarn over").

- Ensure the yarn is hooked onto the groove of the crochet hook.

4. Pull Through:

- Gently pull the hook with the yarn through the loop that was already on the hook.

- Now, you have completed one chain stitch (ch)!

5. Repeat:

- Continue the yarn over (yo) and pull-through process for as many chain stitches (ch) as your project requires.

- Remember to maintain consistent tension on the yarn for even-sized chain stitches (ch).

Count Your Chains:

Regularly count your chain stitches (ch), especially if your project requires a specific number of chains (ch). The slip knot at the beginning does not count as a stitch.

Practice:

Make chain stitches (ch) until you feel comfortable and can produce even and consistent stitches.

Beginner Tips:

- This chain is the base for crochet projects such as garments, blankets, or crocheted pieces.

- Adjust hook size or yarn type according to project requirements and desired fabric density.

- This foundational skill is crucial for all crochet projects.

Common Mistakes

Even the simplest stitch can be tricky at first. Here are a few common mishaps and how to fix them:

- Chains Too Tight: If your chain stitches are so tight you struggle to insert the hook into them for the next row, you're likely holding the yarn too taut. Try relaxing your grip on the yarn and hook, allowing the yarn to flow more freely.

- Inconsistent Size: If your chains vary widely, it's often due to uneven yarn tension. Practice maintaining a steady tension, and don't be afraid to undo (or "frog") your work and try again. Remember, crochet is as much about the process as the end product.

- Losing Count: It's easy to lose track of how many chains you've made, especially in projects requiring a long foundation chain. Try placing stitch markers or small pieces of a different colored yarn every 20 stitches to keep count without losing your place.

With its simplicity and versatility, the chain stitch is the first step in your crochet adventure. The thread connects your intentions to your creations, a reminder that great things can grow from small beginnings. As you practice and become more comfortable with this fundamental stitch, you'll find it's not just about making loops but about laying the groundwork for all the beautiful projects yet to come in your crochet journey.

5.2 Slip Stitch: The Invisible Seam of Crochet

Often underrated, the slip stitch possesses a quiet elegance, serving roles that stretch far beyond its initial impression. With its minimalistic approach, this stitch can transform the surface of crochet work, adding layers of texture and complexity with a subtlety that belies its simplicity.

More Than Joining

While many know the slip stitch as the go-to for connecting crochet pieces or rounds, its potential extends into the realm of design and texture within a single piece. Picture a tapestry of crochet, where the slip stitch acts not just as a thread joining two pieces but as a brushstroke, adding depth and detail. This stitch can create raised lines across the fabric, delineating shapes or adding a tactile dimension to otherwise flat surfaces. It's like drawing on your crochet work, where the slip stitch becomes the pen in your hand.

For those intrigued by the idea of integrating slip stitches into their work, consider starting with simple geometric patterns. Straight lines, circles, or even waves can dramatically alter a project's appearance, turning a basic scarf or blanket into a piece that catches the eye and invites touch.

Surface Crochet

Surface crochet is where the slip stitch truly shines, allowing for adding color and texture without the bulk of additional layers. This technique involves working slip stitches on top of completed crochet fabric, creating patterns or images that stand out against the background. It's akin to embroidery but worked with a crochet hook and the same yarns you've been using, ensuring a perfect match in weight and texture.

To dive into surface crochet, start with a finished project that feels like it could use something extra - a plain beanie, a basic tote bag, or even a set of coasters. With a contrasting color, work slip stitches along the surface, following a pre-drawn design or free-handing as you go. The beauty of surface crochet lies in its flexibility - mistakes are easily undone, and the possibilities are as limitless as your imagination.

Tightness and Tension

Managing tension is one of the trickiest aspects of working with slip stitches, mainly when used for surface crochet or as a design element within a piece. Too tight, and the fabric puckers, pulling at the surrounding stitches and distorting the overall appearance. Too loose, and the slip stitches lack definition, blending into the background when they should stand out.

Finding the proper tension for slip stitches requires a bit of practice. Try working a few practice rows on a swatch, adjusting your grip and the yarn's tension until the stitches lie flat against the fabric but retain their shape and definition. Remember, the slip stitch's subtlety is part of its charm - it should complement, not compete with, the existing crochet work.

Step-by-Step Slip Stitch Instructions

Materials:

- Yarn of choice (cotton worsted weight #4 (medium) is very popular)

- Crochet hook suitable for your yarn (H-8/5mm is a very popular size)

- Scissors

- Yarn needle (for weaving in ends)

Abbreviations Used:

ch = chain

dc = half double crochet

yo = yarn over

US: slip stitch (sl st) ~ UK: slip stitch (sl st, ss) ~ Spanish: punto enano (pe)

Special thanks to Renate Kirkpatrick for the beautiful stitch illustrations - Ren's Fibre Art
https://rensfibreart.wordpress.com/handy-crochet-tips-tricks-2/stitch-overview/

1. Creating a Foundation Chain (If starting from scratch):

- Yarn Over (yo): With the slip knot on your hook, wrap the yarn over your hook from back to front.

- Pull Through: Pull this yarn through the slip knot loop on your hook, creating your first chain (ch).

- Repeat: Continue this process (yo and pull through) for the desired number of chains. This chain of stitches will serve as the foundation for your work.

2. Insert Hook:

- Insert your hook into the second chain from the hook. You can identify the chains by counting the loops starting from the hook.

3. Yarn Over:

- Yarn over your hook (wrap the yarn around the hook from back to front).

4. Pull Through:

- Pull the yarn through the stitch you inserted your hook into, then through the loop on your hook. This completes one slip stitch.

5. Repeat:

- Repeat steps 3 to 5 for each chain stitch in your foundation chain until you reach the end.

Finishing Your Work:

Once you've completed your slip stitches, cut the yarn, leaving a few inches of tail. Yo and pull the yarn completely through the last loop on your hook. Pull tight to secure.

Tips for Success:

- Keep Even Tension: Try to maintain a consistent yarn tension to ensure your stitches are even and not too tight or loose.

- Practice: If new to crochet, practice making chains and slip stitches on scrap yarn to get comfortable with the motions and tension.

- Patience: Learning to crochet takes time. Be patient with yourself, and don't hesitate to unravel and try again.

- Use for Seaming: Slip stitches are great for joining crochet pieces together because they create a flat, almost invisible seam.

- Use for Edging: Slip stitches create a simple finished edge around a project.

- Movement Across the Fabric: If you need to move your yarn and hook to another part of your crochet fabric without creating height, you can use slip stitches to traverse the area invisibly.

5.3 Single Crochet: The Building Block Stitch

The single crochet stitch, in its simplicity, holds the potential to create an astonishing range of textures and forms. It's akin to the humble grain of sand that, under the right conditions, transforms into a luminous pearl. This stitch, approachable and straightforward, serves as the canvas upon which countless crochet projects come to life. From the cozy warmth of a baby blanket to the structured elegance of a tote bag, the single crochet adapts, proving its worth as a true cornerstone of the craft.

The Versatility of Single Crochet

The adaptability of the single crochet stitch is nothing short of remarkable. It seamlessly fits into various projects, making it a reliable choice for beginners and seasoned artisans. Consider the dense fabric it creates when worked in rows, perfect for dishcloths that see daily use or potholders that protect hands from heat. Yet, with a slight variation in yarn or hook size, it lends itself to the delicate openness needed for a spring scarf or the sides of a breezy, beach-ready tote. This stitch alone can form the basis of entire projects or serve as a fundamental building block in more complex patterns, showcasing its unparalleled versatility. The single crochet stitch is one of the most fundamental stitches in crochet.

Step-by-Step Single Crochet Instructions

Materials:

- Yarn of choice (cotton worsted weight #4 (medium) is very popular)

- Crochet hook suitable for your yarn (H-8/5mm is a very popular size)

- Scissors

- Yarn needle (for weaving in ends)

Abbreviations Used:

ch = chain

tch = turning chain

sc = single crochet

yo = yarn over

yoh = yarn over hook

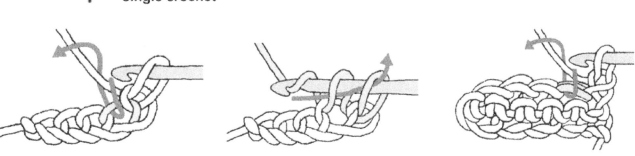

US: single crochet (dc)~ UK: double crochet (sc) ~ Spanish: punto bajo (pb)

Special thanks to Renate Kirkpatrick for the beautiful stitch illustrations - Ren's Fibre Art
https://rensfibreart.wordpress.com/handy-crochet-tips-tricks-2/stitch-overview/

1. Making the Foundation Chain:

- Start by creating a slip knot on your crochet hook.

- Chain (ch) the number of stitches required by your pattern. This initial series of chain (ch) stitches forms the foundation for your project.

- You can work into the chain in two ways: Into the center of the V in the stitch or into what is referred to as the "back bump" of the chain. Practice both ways to find out what you like best.

2. Beginning Your First Single Crochet:

- Look at the chain (ch) stitches you've made; counting from the hook, skip the first chain (ch) stitch.

- Insert your crochet hook into the center of the next chain (ch) stitch (the second chain from your hook).

3. Yarn Over:

- Bring the yarn over hook (yoh) from the back towards you to the front.

4. Pulling Up a Loop:

- With the yarn over hook (yoh), gently pull the hook back through the chain stitch (ch) where it was inserted.

- You should now see two loops on your hook.

5. Yarning Over Again:

- Wrap the yarn over hook (yoh) once more, moving from back to front.

6. Completing the Stitch:

- Pull this yarn through both loops on your crochet hook.

- Congratulations, you've just made a single crochet (sc) stitch!

Continuing Across the Foundation Chain:

- Move to the next chain (ch) stitch along your foundation chain.

- Repeat the process of inserting the hook, yarning over (yo), pulling up a loop, yarning over (yo) again, and pulling through both loops on the hook for each chain (ch) stitch across the foundation.

Starting a New Row:

- Once you've reached the end of your foundation chain and completed the last single crochet (sc), it's time to start a new row.

- Chain (ch) one stitch. This acts as your turning chain (tch).

- Turn your work so the row you've just completed faces you and is ready to be worked back across.

Beginning the New Row:

- Skip the very first chain (ch) stitch directly below the turning chain (tch) you just made.

- Insert your crochet hook into the first stitch of the previous row (not the turning chain).

- Repeat the single crochet (sc) steps (3 through 6) for each stitch across this new row.

Continuing Your Project:

Repeat the process of chaining one, turning your work, and working single crochet (sc) stitches across each row for as many rows as your project requires.

Finishing:

- Once your project reaches the desired size, cut the yarn, leaving a tail.

- Yarn over (yo) and pull through the last loop on your hook to fasten off.

- Weave in ends with a yarn needle.

Practice:

Practice making single crochet (sc) stitches until you feel comfortable producing them evenly. This stitch is the building block for many patterns and projects, such as dishcloths, scarves, and more, so mastering it will give you a solid foundation in crochet.

Consistent Tension:

Maintaining an even tension on the yarn for uniform stitches is essential. The fabric created by single crochet (sc) stitches should be firm but not too tight.

Tension and Evenness

The beauty of a single crochet fabric lies in its uniformity, a quality achieved through consistent tension. The even pull on the yarn as it flows through your fingers and wraps around the hook ensures each stitch is the same size as its neighbors.

Here are a few tips to maintain this consistency:

- Hold the yarn in a manner that feels natural yet allows you to adjust the tension easily. This might involve winding the yarn around your fingers or using a yarn guide.

- Practice maintaining a relaxed grip on both the yarn and the hook. Tension in your hands translates to tension in your stitches.

- Pay attention to the rhythm of your crocheting. A steady pace helps keep tension uniform.

Troubleshooting Common Problems

Even the most experienced crocheters encounter challenges with single crochet stitches from time to time. Here's how you can address some of the most common issues:

- Stitches too Tight: If inserting your hook into a stitch is difficult, loosen your grip on the yarn and hook. Consider using a larger hook size to practice until you find a comfortable tension.

- Stitches too Loose: This often results from holding the yarn too loosely or using a hook much larger than the yarn weight recommends. Experiment with tightening your grip on the yarn or switching to a smaller hook.

- Uneven Edges: This problem usually occurs when stitches at the beginning or end of rows are missed or added accidentally. Counting your stitches at the end of each row can help avoid this. Using stitch markers at the start and end of rows can also serve as a helpful reminder.

5.4 Half Double Crochet: The In-Betweener Stitch

Nestled comfortably between the concise single crochet and the lofty double crochet, the half double crochet stitch (hdc) stands out as a harmonious blend of both. This stitch, with its unique positioning, offers a dense and flexible texture, making it a favorite for crocheters seeking a fabric that's rich in texture yet retains a soft drape. This versatility allows the half double crochet to adapt seamlessly to various projects, from garments that hug the body with gentle warmth to easily-flow accessories.

Balancing Act

The half double crochet does more than fill a gap in stitch heights; it creates a balance in the fabric's structure. This stitch achieves a height perfect for projects where the single crochet might feel too tight and the double crochet too open. It's like finding that sweet spot in music where the rhythm is just right - not too fast or slow. The half double crochet offers a solution that combines the solidity of single crochet stitches with the flexibility and speed of double crochet stitches, making it an indispensable tool in the crocheter's kit.

The half-double crochet stitch is known for creating a semi-tight fabric with a bit more flexibility and texture than a single crochet. This makes it a great choice for sweaters, hats, scarves, and blankets. Enjoy experimenting with this stitch in your crochet projects!

Step-by-Step Half Double Crochet Instructions

Materials:

- Yarn of choice (cotton worsted weight #4 (medium) is very popular)

- Crochet hook suitable for your yarn (H-8/5mm is a very popular size)

- Scissors

- Yarn needle (for weaving in ends)

Abbreviations Used:

ch = chain

hdc = half double crochet

yo = yarn over

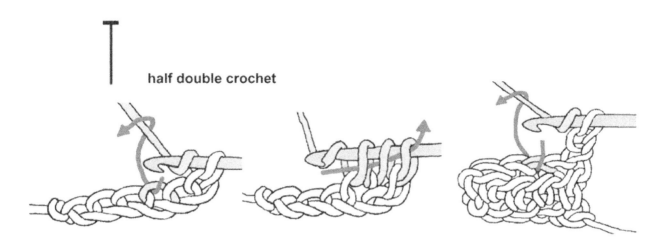

US: half double crochet (hdc) ~UK: half treble (htr)~ Spanish: punto alto (pa)

Special thanks to Renate Kirkpatrick for the beautiful stitch illustrations - Ren's Fibre Art
https://rensfibreart.wordpress.com/handy-crochet-tips-tricks-2/stitch-overview/

1. Start with a Foundation Chain:

You will begin with the required number of chain (ch) stitches according to your pattern, which will serve as the base for your project.

2. Yarn Over:

Yarn over (yo) from back to front before inserting the hook into the stitch.

3. Insert the Hook:

Insert your crochet hook into the third chain from the hook for the first row. The two chains you skip provide the necessary height for your first half double crochet stitch.

4. Yarn Over Again and Pull Up a Loop:

After inserting the hook into the chain, yarn over (yo) again and pull the yarn back through the chain stitch. Your hook should now have three loops.

5. Yarn Over and Pull Through All Three Loops:

Yarn over (yo) once more, and then pull this loop through all three loops on your hook in one go. You have now completed one half double crochet (hdc) stitch.

Repeat Across the Chain:

Continue the process (steps 2 to 5) in each chain across your foundation chain. Remember to yarn over (yo) before inserting the hook into each new stitch.

Starting New Rows:

- To begin a new row after reaching the end, chain (ch) two (this counts as the first half double crochet of the new row), then turn your work to start the next row.

- Yarn over (yo), insert the hook into the first stitch from the hook (not counting the turning chain as a stitch), and repeat the process for each stitch across the row.

Repeat for Additional Rows:

Continue creating as many rows as needed for your project, always starting each new row with a chain two, which provides the height for the half double crochet stitches in the new row.

Maintain Even Tension:

Try maintaining consistent tension on the yarn for uniformed half double crochet (hdc) stitches. Adjusting your grip on the yarn and hook can help you find a comfortable tension that suits your style.

Practice:

Practice making half-double crochet (hdc) stitches until you feel comfortable with them and can produce even and consistent stitches. This stitch is so versatile that it can be used in a variety of projects.

Texture and Flexibility

The half-double crochet stitch contributes a texture to the fabric that is noticeably more pronounced than a single crochet but less bulky than a double crochet. This stitch strikes a perfect chord of flexibility, making it ideal for pieces that require a soft, yielding structure with a hint of firmness. Think of a cozy hat that needs to maintain its shape but still feels soft against the skin or a baby blanket that's warm without being too heavy. The half-double crochet stitch achieves this by creating a compact yet supple fabric that holds defined shapes while embracing the gentle contours of whatever it adorns.

5.5 Double Trouble: Mastering the Double Crochet Stitch

The double crochet stitch is your go-to when you're ready to add height and airiness to your crochet projects. This stitch, slightly taller than its single and half double cousins, offers a delightful blend of versatility and texture, making it perfect for everything from cozy blankets to delicate lace garments. Its open, lofty structure works quickly, satisfying those who love to see rapid progress in their creations.

Step-by-Step Double Crochet Stitch Instructions

Materials:

- Yarn of choice (cotton worsted weight #4 (medium) is very popular)

- Crochet hook suitable for your yarn (H-8/5mm is a very popular size)

- Scissors

- Yarn needle (for weaving in ends)

Abbreviations Used:

ch = chain

dc = double crochet

yo = yarn over

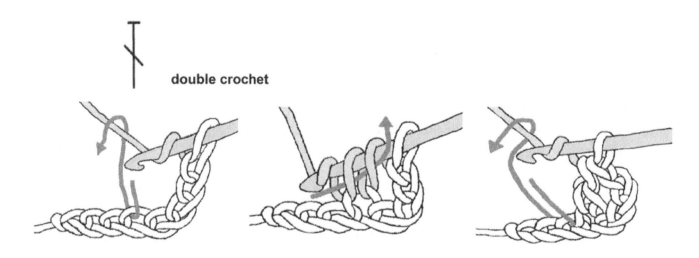

double crochet

US: double crochet (dc) ~ UK: treble (tr) ~ Spanish: punto alto doble (pad)

Special thanks to Renate Kirkpatrick for the beautiful stitch illustrations - Ren's Fibre Art
https://rensfibreart.wordpress.com/handy-crochet-tips-tricks-2/stitch-overview/

1. Start with a Foundation Chain:

Begin with the number of chain (ch) stitches your pattern requires. Remember, the foundation chain serves as the base for your project.

2. Yarn Over:

To start your first double crochet (dc), yarn over (yo) (wrap the yarn around your crochet hook from back to front) before inserting the hook into the stitch.

3. Insert the Hook:

For the first row, insert your crochet hook into the fourth chain from the hook. The first three chains you skip count as your first double crochet stitch.

4. Yarn Over Again and Pull Up a Loop:

After inserting the hook into the correct chain, yarn over (yo) again and then pull the yarn through the chain (ch) stitch. You should now have three loops on your hook.

5. Yarn Over and Pull Through Two Loops:

Yarn over (yo) once more, and then pull the yarn through the first two loops on your hook. You will now have two loops remaining on your hook.

6. Yarn Over and Pull Through the Remaining Two Loops:

Yarn over (yo) again and draw the yarn through the remaining two loops on your hook. You've now completed one double crochet (dc) stitch.

Continue the Double Crochet Stitches Across:

Repeat steps 2 to 6 in each chain (ch) across your foundation chain for the first row. Remember to yarn over (yo) before inserting the hook into each new stitch.

Starting New Rows:

- After you reach the end, you'll need to turn your work to begin a new row. Chain (ch) three stitches (this counts as the first double crochet of the new row), then turn your work to start the next row.

- Yarn over (yo) and insert the hook into the second stitch from the hook (not counting the turning chain as a stitch), then repeat the process (steps 4 to 6) for each stitch across the row.

Repeat for Additional Rows:

Continue creating as many rows as needed for your project, always starting each new row with a chain of three (which counts as the first double crochet), then turning your work and proceeding with double crochet (dc) stitches into each stitch across.

Practice:

The double crochet stitch can be used in various projects, from blankets to garments. Practice making even and consistent double crochet stitches.

As we wrap up this exploration of foundational crochet stitches and techniques, we're reminded of the craft's inherent beauty and versatility. From the foundational chain stitch that sets the stage to the slip stitch that adds finishing touches, each technique we've covered offers a unique contribution to the tapestry of crochet. These stitches are the building blocks upon which all crochet projects are built, each with the potential to create, embellish, and transform.

Help Me Make a Difference with Your Review

"Happiness doesn't result from what we get, but from what we give."
–Ben Carson

Unlock the Power of Generosity

Hey there! Would you join me in spreading the joy of crochet to others? Your opinion can make a world of difference!

Just imagine - with a few simple clicks, you can help fellow crafters discover the wonderful world of crochet and experience the same joy and relaxation you found within these pages.

Crochet isn't just about yarn and hooks; it's about unlocking your creativity, finding solace in every stitch, and connecting with a community as warm and welcoming as your favorite blanket. And I've been here every step of the way, guiding you through this delightful journey.

This book is for everyone, whether you're young or young at heart, brand new to crochet, or rediscovering an old hobby. With clear illustrations and easy-to-follow instructions, I aim to make learning crochet stress-free and fun. Think of me as your crochet buddy, here to ensure your journey is as enjoyable as possible!

Now, let's make a difference together! Sharing your thoughts on this book will help others find their creative outlet and embark on their crochet adventures.

Thank you for your generosity and support. Your review can brighten someone's day and inspire them to pick up a hook and yarn. Please take 60 seconds to kindly leave a review on Amazon. Let's spread happiness, one stitch at a time!

Simply scan the QR code to leave your review:
1. Open your camera on your phone
2. Hover it over the QR code
3. Rate/review my book

Or visit this link to leave a review:
https://www.amazon.com/review/review-your-purchases/?asin=B0D73GHSPY

With heartfelt gratitude,
Ella Knotsley

PS - Did you know that sharing something valuable with another person makes you more valuable to them? If you think this book will help a fellow crocheter, why not pass it along?

Chapter 6

Elevating Your Crochet with Textured Stitches

*** Please scan the QR code to view the projects and images in color ***

Picture this: a cozy blanket draped over a couch, a scarf wrapped snugly around a loved one, a custom purse slung over a shoulder. What elevates these items from simple crochet pieces to standout creations? Texture. This chapter delves into the world of textured stitches, starting with the popcorn stitch. This stitch adds a delightful, tactile dimension to projects, transforming them from flat to fabulously 3D.

6.1 Popcorn Stitch: Adding Texture to Your Projects

Much like its namesake, the popcorn stitch pops from the fabric, creating little bursts of texture that beg to be touched. It combines the simple mechanics of basic stitches with a clever little twist to create a pronounced texture. Ideal for those who want to add depth to their work, this stitch is surprisingly straightforward but packs a punch in visual and tactile appeal.

Creating Popcorn Stitches

Materials:

- Cotton or acrylic worsted weight #4 (medium) yarns in various colors for temperature ranges

- Size H-8 (5mm) crochet hook

- Scissors

- Yarn needle (for weaving in ends)

Abbreviations Used:

ch = chain

sc = single crochet

dc = double crochet

pc = popcorn stitch

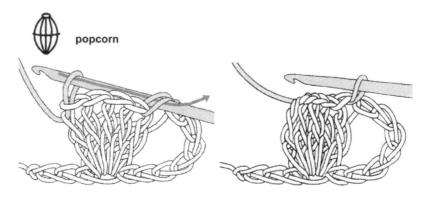

US: popcorn (PC)~ UK: popcorn (PC)~ Spanish: puntos altos cerrados juntas / con una cadeneta

Special thanks to Renate Kirkpatrick for the beautiful stitch illustrations - Ren's Fibre Art
https://rensfibreart.wordpress.com/handy-crochet-tips-tricks-2/stitch-overview/

Foundation:

- Begin with a foundation chain (ch) of your desired length.

- Depending on your project needs, complete a base row in single crochet (sc) or double crochet (dc).

Popcorn Stitch (pc) Instructions:

Start Popcorn Stitch: In the next stitch where you want the popcorn stitch (pc) to appear, work 5 double crochets (dc) into the same stitch.

1. Drop Loop: After completing the 5 dc, drop the loop from your hook. Be careful not to unravel your work.

2. Insert Hook: Insert your hook from front to back through the top of the first dc of the 5-dc group.

3. Pick Up Dropped Loop: With your hook in place, grab the dropped loop and pull it through the first dc.

4. Secure the Popcorn: Chain (ch) 1 to secure the popcorn stitch. This completes one popcorn stitch (pc).

Continuing Your Project:

- Continue with your pattern until you reach the next point where a popcorn stitch (pc) is desired. Repeat the instructions for each popcorn stitch.

- After completing all popcorn stitches (pc) for the row, continue with the pattern or stitch specified in your project instructions.

Additional Tips:

- Popcorn stitches can significantly texture your fabric, making them ideal for decorative elements in blankets, hats, scarves, and more.

- To keep your work even, maintain consistent tension, especially when creating the 5 dc for each popcorn stitch.

- The securing chain (ch 1) does not count as a stitch in the subsequent row unless specified by your pattern.

Finishing Your Work:

- Once you've completed your project with the desired number of popcorn stitches, finish off by weaving in all ends with a yarn needle for a neat appearance.

- Blankets: Incorporate popcorn stitches in baby blankets for a tactile exploration or in afghans as a decorative element. Spacing out the popcorn stitches can create a starry night effect, perfect for cozy evenings.

- Scarves: Add popcorn stitches along the edges of a scarf for a fun, textured border, or intersperse them throughout for a touch of whimsy.

- Purses: Work popcorn stitches into the flap of a crocheted purse for a chic, textured look that stands out.

- Alternate rows of popcorn stitches with basic crochet stitches for a quilted effect. This technique adds warmth and visual interest to blankets and cushions.

Fixing Mistakes

- If a popcorn stitch doesn't pop, check if you've worked the correct number of double crochets. Five is usually the magic number for a pronounced texture.

- Accidentally skipping the step where you pull the loop through the first double crochet can result in a cluster that doesn't stand out. Simply undo the chain stitch, secure the popcorn, and redo the finishing steps.

- Uneven popcorn stitches often result from inconsistent tension. Practice maintaining a steady yarn tension, and remember that it's okay to redo stitches to achieve uniformity.

As a popcorn stitch or another technique, texture brings a new dimension to crochet projects. It adds interest, depth, and a tactile quality that can transform a simple piece into something extraordinary. As you explore these textured stitches, remember that each pop, loop, and stitch is an opportunity to infuse your creations with personality and style. With its playful roundness and 3D effect, the popcorn stitch is just the beginning of what you can achieve when you add texture to your crochet repertoire.

6.2 Shell Stitch: Creating Waves and Edges

With its delicate arcs and soft curves, the shell stitch introduces an oceanic tranquility to crochet projects. This stitch can mimic the rhythmic waves of the sea or the gentle outlines of seashells, bringing a piece of the beach into your home or wardrobe. Here's how you can incorporate this versatile stitch into your crochet work, adding a splash of elegance and a hint of nostalgia for coastal adventures.

Shell Stitch Basics

Creating a shell stitch involves working multiple stitches into a single base stitch, causing them to fan out and make a shell-like appearance. The beauty of this stitch lies in its simplicity and the instant texture it adds to any project.

Special thanks to Crochet with Gabriella Rose for the Sunset Shore Blanket image. The free Sunset Shore Blanket pattern can be found on the website crochetwithgabriellarose.com. You can also find Crochet with Gabriella Rose on Instagram @crochetwithgabriellarose

Creating Shell Stitches

Materials:

- Cotton or acrylic worsted weight #4 (medium) yarns in various colors for temperature ranges

- Size H-8 (5mm) crochet hook

- Scissors

- Yarn needle (for weaving in ends)

Abbreviations Used:

ch = chain

dc = double crochet

tch = turning chain

sh = shell stitch

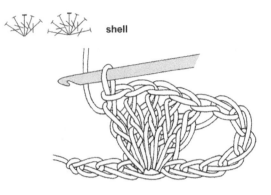

UK: shell (sh)~ US: shell (sh)

Special thanks to Renate Kirkpatrick for the beautiful stitch illustrations –
Ren's Fibre Art
https://rensfibreart.wordpress.com/handy-crochet-tips-tricks-2/stitch-ove
rview/

Start with a Foundation Chain:

- Create a slip knot on your hook.

- Chain (ch) a multiple of 6 stitches plus an additional 1 stitch for the turning chain (tch). For example, chain (ch) 19 (6 x 3 + 1).

Row 1:

- Single Crochet (sc): Make 1 single crochet (sc) in the second chain from the hook.

- Skip and Shell: Skip the next 2 chains (ch), then make 5 double crochets (dc) in the next chain (ch). This creates the "shell."

- Repeat: Skip the next 2 chains (ch), make 1 single crochet (sc) in the next chain (ch) . Continue this pattern across the row.

- End of Row: After the last shell, skip 2 chains (ch) and make 1 single crochet (sc) in the last chain. Chain (ch) 3 and turn your work.

Row 2:

- Start with a Shell (sh): Make 2 double crochets (dc) in the first single crochet (sc) (this counts as half of a shell).

- SC in Shell: Make 1 single crochet (sc) in the center of the next shell (sh)(the 3rd double crochet (dc) of the 5).

- Shell in SC: Make 5 double crochets (dc) in the next single crochet (sc).

- Repeat: Continue this pattern across the row.

- End of Row: After the last single crochet (sc), make 3 double crochets (dc) in the top of the turning chain (tch) from the previous row. Chain (ch) 1 and turn your work.

Row 3:

- Single Crochet: Make 1 single crochet (sc) in the first double crochet (dc).

- Shell in SC: Make 5 double crochets (dc) in the next single crochet (sc).

- Repeat: Continue this pattern across the row.

- End of Row: After the last shell (sh), make 1 single crochet (sc) in the top of the turning chain (tch) from the previous row. Chain 3 and turn your work.

Continue the Pattern:

- Repeat Rows 2 and 3 until your project reaches the desired length.

Finishing:

Once you reach the desired size of your project, fasten off the yarn and weave in all ends with a yarn needle for a neat finish.

Edge Creation

Shell stitches excel in adding decorative edges to projects. Their natural scalloping creates a finished look that's both refined and charming. To edge a blanket or garment with shell stitches:

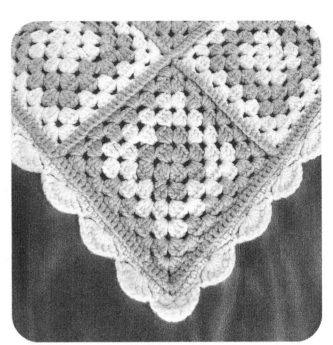

- Start at one corner or end of your project, ensuring the base edge has a stitch count compatible with your shell stitch pattern.

- If your project doesn't already have one, work a row of single crochet stitches. This provides a smooth base for your shells.

- Begin your shell stitch edging into the spaces between the single crochets. This technique gives your edge a clean, even appearance.

- For corners, you may need to adjust the number of stitches in your shell or work additional stitches to maintain the project's shape.

Design Patterns

Incorporating shell stitches into larger projects opens up a world of design possibilities. The shell stitch adapts to your creative vision, from airy summer tops that breathe with every stitch to plush throws that invite cozy evenings.

Consider these ideas:

- A Chevron Throw: Alternate rows of shell stitches with rows of single crochet decreases to create a chevron pattern. The peaks and valleys formed by the shells add a tactile dimension that's visually striking and comforting to the touch.

- A Lace Shawl: Use shell stitches in varying sizes to create a delicate, lace-like fabric. The natural gaps between shells provide an elegant and lightweight openwork effect, perfect for evening wear or as a bridal accessory.

Adjusting Shell Size

Adapting the shell stitch to different yarn weights and project types is straightforward once you understand the basics. The key lies in adjusting the number of stitches in each shell:

- For Thinner Yarns: Decrease the number of stitches in each shell. Working three or four double crochets can produce a delicate shell that complements the lighter weight of the yarn.

- For Bulkier Yarns: Increase the number of stitches to six or more. The added volume helps maintain the shell's definition and texture, even with thicker yarns.

- For Different Projects: Consider the scale of your project. A blanket might benefit from larger, more pronounced shells, while a scarf or hat might look best with smaller, subtler shells.

Experimenting with different shell sizes allows you to customize your projects and play with texture and scale, adding a personal touch to your creations.

As we wrap up this exploration, it's evident that the crochet world offers endless possibilities for personalization and artistic expression. Each project becomes a canvas for creativity by introducing textured stitches, reflecting the maker's personality and vision. With these tools and techniques at your disposal, the journey from basic stitches to intricate, personalized creations is not just possible but filled with moments of joy and discovery.

Chapter 7

Quick Wins

SIMPLE PROJECTS FOR ABSOLUTE BEGINNERS

*** Please scan the QR code to view the projects and images in color ***

C rocheting can sometimes feel like trying to solve a Rubik's Cube. It's all fun and games until you can't determine the next move. But what if there was a project so simple yet gratifying that it felt like the cube solved itself in your hands?

Enter the humble square coaster. It might not sound like the crown jewel of crochet projects but think of it as the gateway craft. It's your first step into making something practical and pretty, with a sense of accomplishment that's as satisfying as nailing a new recipe on the first try.

Imagine your coffee table adorned with these handmade treasures, a testament to your blossoming skill. Coasters are not just about protecting wood surfaces; they're about adding a personal touch to your space, a splash of color, or a conversation starter when guests notice the unique patterns under their cups. This square coaster project is your crochet "mic drop" - simple yet impactful.

7.1 Making a Square Coaster: Your First Crochet Project

Here's where you roll up your sleeves. You're golden if you've mastered the chain stitch, single crochet, and double crochet from earlier chapters. This square crochet coaster pattern is excellent for practicing single and double crochet stitches. It results in a functional and durable home accessory.

Materials Needed:

- Cotton worsted weight #4 (medium) yarn, approx. 20 yards

- Size H-8 (5 mm) crochet hook

- Scissors

- Yarn needle (for weaving in ends)

Gauge:

It is not important for this pattern

The Importance of Choosing the Right Yarn: Worsted-weight cotton yarn is king for coasters. It's sturdy, absorbent, and washes well - perfect for catching drips and spills.

Step-by-Step Square Coaster Instructions: 4.5" x 4.5"

Abbreviations Used:

ch = chain

sc = single crochet

dc = double crochet

Pattern:

1. Foundation: Start with a Slip Knot and Chain (ch)

- Make a slip knot on your hook.

- Chain (ch) 14 to start (or a number that achieves the desired width, adjusting for yarn weight and hook size).

2. Row 1: Single Crochet (sc)

- Single crochet (sc) in the second chain (ch) from the hook.

- Single crochet (sc) in each chain (ch) across. (13)

- You should have 13 single crochets (sc).

- Chain (ch) 1, then turn your work.

3. Row 2 to Desired Height:

- Single crochet (sc) 1, double crochet 1, repeat across the row. (13)

- At the end of each row, chain (ch) 1 and turn your work.

- Continue repeating rows 1 and 2 for 13 rows, ending with single crochet (sc). To check that your piece is square, fold it diagonally; the edges should meet perfectly to form a triangle if it's square.

Border:

By following these step-by-step instructions, your coaster will not only look more finished but will also hold up better over time, retaining its shape and structure through multiple washes:

- Do Not Cut the Yarn: Continue with the working end of the yarn from your project; this avoids the need to join new yarn and makes the coaster more secure.

- Begin the Border: Chain (ch) 1. This chain (ch) 1 is considered the border's first single crochet (sc).

- Work Single Crochets Around the Edge: Make single crochets (sc) evenly spaced around the entire edge of the coaster. To ensure the stitches are distributed evenly, you might need to adjust the spacing slightly, especially on sides without precise stitches to work into.

- Corners: Work 3 single crochets (sc) in each corner of the coaster. This helps maintain a smooth, rounded corner and prevents the coaster from curling at the edges.

Securing Yarn Tails:

As you crochet around, ensure that you crochet over any yarn tails from the beginning of your project. This method effectively weaves in loose ends as you go, securing them in place and reducing the likelihood of unraveling during use or washes.

Join the Border:

Once you have crocheted 2 rows of sc around the entire coaster, complete the border by joining with a slip stitch to the first chain you made at the beginning of the border.

Finishing Touches:

Cut the yarn, leaving a tail long enough to be woven securely. Use a yarn needle to weave in this end and any other loose ends you might have, ensuring everything is neat.

Tips:

- Ensure consistent tension for even edges.

- Count your stitches occasionally to ensure the coaster remains square.

Square Coaster Pattern In Crochet Terms:

Foundation: Start with a slip knot on your hook. Ch 14 (13 + 1 for turning).

Row 1: Sc in 2nd ch from hook, sc in each ch across, ch 1, and turn. (13 sc)

Row 2: Sc 1, dc 1, repeat across row (13), ch1, and turn.

Repeat Rows 1 and 2- for 13 rows, ending with sc until your piece is square. Check by folding the edges diagonally to form a triangle. Once square, do not chain 1 at the end of your last row.

Border: Without cutting yarn, ch 1 (counts as 1st sc). Sc 2 rows evenly around the project edge, 3 sc in each corner. Sl st to the first ch to join. Cut yarn and weave in ends.

Variations for Practice: It's time to play once you've nailed the basic square coaster. Mix up the colors for a vibrant set. Try different stitches for texture. How about a scalloped edge for flair? These variations are not just about showcasing your skill but also about discovering what you enjoy in crochet. It's like cooking; once you've learned to make a basic sauce, you can experiment with spices and ingredients. Each coaster becomes a little experiment in creativity and technique.

The magic of starting with a square coaster project lies in the simplicity and utility of the end product and in the confidence it builds. You start with yarn and a hook; soon enough, you've created something tangible, practical, and potentially giftable. It's a small project with big rewards, offering the perfect blend of practice and payoff for beginners eager to see their efforts come to life. Plus, it sets the stage for more complex projects, making it an ideal stepping stone in your crochet adventure.

7.2 Washcloth Wonders: Practicing Basic Stitches

Consider the humble washcloth when you're ready to dip your toes into something useful and delightful to create. This project is a fabulous canvas for practicing stitches, and the end product is something everyone can find a use for, from scrubbing dishes to pampering in a spa-like bath.

The beauty of crafting washcloths lies in their immediate gratification; they're quick to complete, making them perfect for those moments when you crave the satisfaction of a finished project without a significant time investment.

Material Selection for Absorbency

The choice of yarn is crucial for washcloths, as it needs to be both absorbent and soft. Cotton and bamboo yarns (medium-worsted weight) are top picks for these projects. Cotton, known for its durability and high absorbency, makes washcloths perfect for kitchen use or as gentle exfoliators for your skin. On the other hand, bamboo brings silky softness to the mix and natural antibacterial properties, making it ideal for face cloths or baby washcloths. Both materials are eco-friendly options that add a touch of luxury to everyday tasks.

Materials Needed:

- Cotton or bamboo worsted weight #4 (medium) is ideal for its absorbency and durability, approx. 90 yards

- Size H-8 (5 mm) crochet hook

- Scissors

- Yarn needle (for weaving in ends)

Gauge:

It is not important for this project

Abbreviations Used:

ch = chain

sc = single crochet

st = stitch(es)

yo = yarn over

Step-by-Step Washcloth Instructions: 8" x 8"

Pattern:

1: Start with a Slip Knot

Create a slip knot on your hook. This is the first step in almost every crochet project and secures your yarn to begin crocheting.

2: Chain Stitches for Width

Chain (ch) 30 stitches. This number will determine the width of your washcloth. For a standard size, 30 chains (ch) create a good starting point, resulting in an approximately 8-inch washcloth. Still, you can adjust this number for a larger or smaller cloth.

3: First Row of Single Crochets (sc)

- Insert your hook into the second chain (ch) from the hook (the first chain is skipped and does not count as a stitch).

- Yarn over (yo) and pull up a loop (two loops on the hook now).

- Yarn over (yo) again and pull through both loops on the hook. This completes one single crochet (sc).

- Continue to single crochet (sc) across each chain. You will have 29 single crochets (sc) for this row.

4: Create Additional Rows

- Chain (ch) 1 (turning chain), then turn your work. This chain (ch) 1 does not count as a stitch.

- Single crochet (sc) in the first stitch and each stitch across the row. (29)

- Repeat this step for every row until your washcloth is square. Creating about 30 rows will typically result in a square washcloth, but you can add or subtract rows to achieve your desired size.

Finishing Your Washcloth

Finishing Options:

Option 1: Fastening Off

- Cut yarn and leave a 6-inch tail.

- Pull the tail through the last loop and tighten.

- Weave in ends with yarn needle.

Option 2: Adding a Border

- Without cutting yarn, ch 1 (counts as 1st sc).

- Sc evenly around the project edge, 3 sc in each corner.

- Sl st to the first ch to join.

- Cut yarn and weave in ends.

Washcloth Pattern In Crochet Terms:

Start: Begin with a slip knot on the hook.

Foundation Row: Ch 30. This sets the width of your washcloth.

Row 1: Sc in 2nd ch from hook and in each ch across row. You will have 29 sc.

Row 2 - End: Ch 1 (does not count as a st), turn your work. Sc in 1st st and each sc across row. Total 29 st(s) in every row. Repeat this row until the washcloth is square, approximately 30 rows; adjust the number of rows for the desired size.

Finishing Options:

Option 1: Fastening Off: Cut yarn and leave a 6-inch tail. Pull the tail through the last loop and tighten. Weave in ends with yarn needle.

Option 2: Adding a Border: Without cutting yarn, ch 1 (counts as 1st sc). Sc evenly around the project edge, 3 sc in each corner. Sl st to the first ch to join. Cut yarn and weave in ends.

Tips:

- Keep your stitches consistent for an even texture. If you notice your stitches are too tight or loose, adjust your grip on the hook or the tension of the yarn.

- Feel free to experiment with colors, using multiple colors to create stripes or a border.

- Washing your finished washcloth before use can help soften the cotton yarn and improve absorbency.

Pattern Choices

The washcloth is your playground for stitch experimentation. Begin with the foundational stitches you've already learned and see how they transform the texture and function of your washcloth. Here are a few pattern ideas to get you started:

- Solid Stitch Washcloth: Single crochet stitches throughout create a dense, durable fabric ideal for heavy-duty scrubbing. This pattern is also excellent for practicing even tension.

- Textured Washcloth: Alternate rows of single crochet and double crochet stitches. This simple variation introduces a subtle texture that's visually appealing and effective for cleaning.

- Lace-Edged Washcloth: Start with a basic square of half-double crochet stitches. Once completed, add an edging of simple lacework by incorporating chain stitches and single crochets in the final round. This approach elevates the washcloth to a decorative item, perfect for gifting.

With each washcloth you complete, you're not just making a practical item; you're honing your skills, familiarizing yourself with how different stitches behave, and learning to read your crochet work. This practice builds a foundation to serve you well in more complex projects.

Edging for Elegance

Adding a crochet edge to a washcloth does more than prevent the sides from curling; it transforms a basic square of fabric into a refined, finished piece. Even the simplest edging can give your washcloth a handcrafted quality that's visually pleasing and a joy to use.

Here are a couple of edging techniques to try:

- Shell Edging: Work 5 double crochet stitches into the same stitch, skip 2, and slip stitch in the next stitch. Repeat this pattern around the perimeter of your washcloth. This edging adds a scalloped border that's especially lovely on washcloths intended as gifts or for guest bathrooms.

- Crab Stitch Edging: Also known as the reverse single crochet (RSC), this stitch creates a cord-like edge that's both decorative and functional. Work single crochet stitches in the opposite direction (from left to right if you're right-handed and right to left if left-handed). This edging is sturdy and adds a professional touch to your washcloth.

Edgings are an opportunity to personalize your project further and experiment with color. Consider using a contrasting color for the edging to frame your washcloth or match it to the primary color for a subtle, sophisticated look.

The act of creating something as simple as a washcloth can be rewarding. It's a project that offers immediate gratification, practical utility, and the chance to play with colors and textures. Whether making them for yourself, as gifts, or as a way to introduce sustainability into your daily routine, washcloths are a perfect project to weave into your crochet practice.

7.3 Bath Pouf: A Fun and Functional Project

Creating a bath pouf from scratch might sound somewhat ambitious if you're just starting to dip your toes into the crochet world. However, this project is an excellent way to level up from flat items to something more three-dimensional and functional. Plus, there's a certain charm in crafting items that serve a purpose in your daily routine, turning a mundane activity like showering into a moment filled with a bit of personal pride.

This simple yet effective project not only yields a practical bathroom accessory but also allows for personalization in colors, making it a perfect handmade gift or a colorful addition to your own bathroom essentials. This project suits those with basic crochet skills.

Selecting Yarn for Wet Conditions

For a bath pouf, the yarn must be more than just pretty - it has to be practical. The ideal choice here is a soft, quick-drying synthetic yarn. These yarns are designed to withstand moisture without becoming soggy or taking forever to dry. Think along the lines of acrylic or nylon; both are resilient when faced with water and maintain their shape and texture even after numerous washes. The key is to look for yarn that feels gentle to the touch since it will be used against your skin. It also has quick-drying properties to prevent it from becoming a breeding ground for mold or mildew.

Assembly and Use

Caring for your pouf is straightforward. Synthetic yarns typically hold up well under machine washing. However, to extend the life of your pouf, a gentle cycle in a lingerie bag is recommended, followed by air drying. This care routine ensures your pouf remains fresh and ready for its next use.

Making a bath pouf provides a useful item. It allows you to practice techniques like working in the round and managing stitch increases, which are transferable to a wide array of future projects. Plus, the satisfaction of using something you made by hand adds a layer of joy to your daily routine, transforming a simple shower into a celebration of your craft.

Materials Needed:

- Polyester or nylon worsted weight #4 (medium) yarn, approx. 155 yards

- Size H-8 (5mm) crochet hook

- Scissors

- Yarn needle (for weaving in ends)

Gauge:

It is not important for this project

Abbreviations Used:

ch = chain

dc = double crochet

sc = single crochet

sl st = slip stitch

st(s) = stitch(es)

Step-by-Step Bath Pouf Instructions:

Pattern:

1. Creating the Hanging Loop:

- Ch (ch) 7.

- Join with a slip stitch to form a ring.

- Ch 40 to 50 (or desired length)

- Slip stitch (sl st) into the ring at the same chain you started the ch 7.

2. Round 1:

- Chain (ch) 1

- Work 25 single crochets (sc) into the ring.

- Slip stitch (sl st) into the first single crochet (sc) to join. (25 single crochet (sc) since the chain (ch) doesn't count as a stitch).

Note: It doesn't matter if there's a hole because you won't see it when it's finished.

3. Round 2:

- Chain (ch) 2 (counts as the first double crochet [dc]), 2 double crochet (dc) into the first stitch

- Work 3 double crochet (dc) into the next stitch and repeat to the last one.

- Join with a slip stitch (sl st) to the top of the first double crochet (dc). (3 x 25 = 75 total stitches)

4. Round 3:

- Continue the pattern by chaining (ch) 2 (count as the first double crochet [dc]) and 2 double crochet (dc) into the first stitch.

- 3 double crochet (dc) into the next stitch, and repeat to the last one.

- Join with a slip stitch (sl st) to the top of the first double crochet (dc). (you can stop here if you're happy with the fullness of the pouf)

(75 x 3 = 225 total stitches)

5. Round 4 (Final Round):

- Chain (ch) 2 (count as the first double crochet [dc]), 2 double crochet (dc)into the first stitch.

- Work 3 double crochet (dc) into the next stitch and repeat to the last one.

- Join with a slip stitch (sl st) to the top of the first double crochet. (225 x 3 = 675 total stitches)

Finishing Touches:

Cut yarn, leaving a tail. Pull the tail through the last loop on your hook and tighten it to secure it. Weave in the end with a yarn needle.

Bath Pouf Pattern Written in Crochet Terms:

Hanging Loop: Ch 7. Join with a slip stitch to form a ring. Ch 40-50 (or desired length). Slip stitch (sl st) into the ring at the same chain you started the ch 7.

Rnd 1: Ch 1. 25 sc into the ring. Sl st into the first sc to join. (25 sc)

Rnd 2: Ch 2 (counts as first dc). 2 dc in 1st st. 3 dc in next st. Repeat 3 dc around. Sl st to top of 1st dc to join. (75 sc)

Rnd 3: Ch 2 (counts as first dc). 2 dc in 1st st. 3 dc in next st. Repeat 3 dc around. Sl st to top of 1st dc to join. (225 sc)

Rnd 4 (Final Rnd): Ch 2 (counts as first dc). 2 dc in 1st st. 3 dc in next st. Repeat 3 dc around. Sl st to top of 1st dc to join. (675 sc)

Finishing:

Cut yarn, leaving a tail. Pull tail through last loop, tighten. Weave in the end with yarn needle.

Tips:

- Adjust the size of your pouf by adding or reducing rounds.

- Ensure your stitches are not too tight so the pouf can be flexible and usable.

*** Now that you're familiar with crochet terms, following a pattern is important, as seen in crochet books and magazines. The next three projects will not include step-by-step instructions.***

7.4 The Classic Granny Square: A Gateway to Larger Projects

Granny squares, those quaint little squares of color that seem to whisper tales of yesteryear, are actually powerhouses in the crochet world. They're not just a nod to the past but a bridge to many creative possibilities. Imagine each square as a pixel; it's a dot of color alone, but together, they form a vibrant tapestry of hues and patterns. This section explores how you can harness the humble granny square to embark on larger, more complex projects, transforming those single squares into stunning creations.

Color Work Introduction

Diving into colorwork with granny squares is comparable to stepping into a painter's studio. The palette is yours to command, and the squares are your canvas. Here's where you learn the dance of changing yarn colors, a skill that elevates your crochet from monochrome to a kaleidoscope of shades. Start with selecting a set of colors; two to four shades can balance harmony and contrast. As you work on a square, introduce a new color at the beginning of a round. Tie the new color to the old one with a small knot and continue your stitches, weaving in the ends later. This practice adds visual interest to your squares. It builds your confidence in managing multiple yarns, an invaluable technique in many crochet projects.

To ensure smooth color transitions, choose colors that complement each other well. For a subtle ombre effect, you might opt for different shades of the same color or contrasting colors for a bold statement.

Creating a crochet granny square is a classic project for beginners and experienced crocheters alike. It can be used to make blankets, bags, and more. Experiment with yarn colors and sizes to personalize your creations. Enjoy making your granny square! They are a fun, quick project that can be used in many ways. Here's how to make a simple granny square.

Materials Needed:

- Cotton or acrylic worsted weight #4 (medium) yarn in one or more colors, approx. 32 yards per granny square.

- Size H-8 (5mm) crochet hook

- Scissors

- Yarn Needle (for weaving in ends)

Gauge:

It is not important for this project

Abbreviations Used:

ch = chain

sp = space

dc = double crochet

sl st = slip stitch

st(s) = stitch(es)

rep = repeat

* = repeat

Granny Square Pattern:

The granny square can be made all in one color or changed to a different color for each row or every couple of rows. See the notation below for changing colors.

Base ring: Ch4, sl st in 1st ch.

Rnd 1: Ch 5 (counts as 1 dc and ch 2 at the beginning of each round) *3 dc into ring, ch 3, rep from * 2 times, 2 dc into ring, sl st in 3rd ch of ch 5.

Rnd 2: Sl st in next ch, ch 5, 3 dc in same sp * ch 1, skip 3 dc (3 dc, ch 2, 3 dc) in next sp, rep from * 2 times, ch 1, skip 3 sts, 2 dc in same space as ch 5 at start of rnd,

sl st in 3rd ch of ch 5.

Rnd 3: Sl st in next ch, ch 5, 3 dc in same sp * ch 1, skip 3 dc, 3 dc in next space, ch 1, skip 3 dc, (3 dc, ch 2, 3 dc) in next sp, rep from * 2 times then to ch 1 skip 3 dc, 3 dc in next sp, ch 1, skip 3 dc, 2 dc in same space as ch 5 at start of rnd, sl st in 3rd ch of ch 5.

Rnd 4: Sl st in next ch, ch 5, 3 dc in same sp *(ch 1, skip 3 dc, 3 dc in next sp) 2 times, ch 1 skip 3 dc (3dc, ch 2, 3 dc) in next sp, rep from * 2 times, (ch 1, skip 3 dc, 3 dc in next sp) 2 times, ch 1, skip 3 dc, 2 dc in same sp as ch 5 at start of rnd, sl st in 3rd ch of ch 5.

Rnd 5 & 6 are worked the same way. Starting with Sl st in next ch, ch 5, 3 dc in same sp then (ch 1, skip 3 dc, 3 dc in each sp) until you get to the corner, then (3dc, ch 2, 3 dc) in corner, rep until you come to the end of the rnd, finish with 2 dc in same space as ch 5 at start of rnd, sl st in 3rd ch of ch 5.

To finish off, cut your yarn 4 inches from your work toward the working end, then pull that yarn through the loop on your hook. With your yarn needle or hook, weave the tail through the stitches of your granny square.

Tips:

- The initial ch 5 at the start of each round counts as one dc.

- Adjust the size of your square by adding or subtracting the number of rounds.

- Make sure to keep your stitches consistent for a uniform look.

If you wish to make the square larger, continue adding rnds until you have the desired size. If you want the square smaller, subtract rnds.

To change colors: When you have finished a rnd and want to change color, simply cut your yarn 4 inches from your work toward the working end, then pull that yarn through the loop on your hook.

To add your new color: Make your loop on the hook. Sl st over the last sl st you made with the previous color, ch 5, and continue on with the pattern crocheting over the tail of your new color to hide it for the next 3 dc. The rest of the tail can be woven into your square once it's completed.

Joining Techniques

Once you have a stack of colorful granny squares, the next step is to unite them into a larger piece. Several methods exist, each offering a different aesthetic and texture for the final project. The granny square pictured in this book was joined with a slip stitch, as seen by the raised edge.

- **Slip Stitch Join**: The slip stitch join is ideal for a raised, ridge-like seam that adds texture to your project. Use your crochet hook to slip stitch the edges of the squares together, working from the wrong side to keep the ridge discreet.

- **Whip Stitch**: This method involves sewing the squares together using a yarn needle. It creates a nearly invisible seam, perfect for projects where you want the squares to blend seamlessly.

- **Join As You Go**: This technique allows you to connect squares while working the final round of each square. It saves time and yarn, creating a cohesive fabric as you progress.

Experimenting with these joining methods can significantly impact the look and feel of your final project, offering a chance to customize your work further.

Versatility of Granny Squares

The real magic of granny squares lies in their versatility. From traditional Afghans to trendy bags, these squares can be morphed into almost any type of project.

- Blankets and Throws: Perhaps the most iconic use of granny squares, blankets, and throws offers a cozy way to showcase your work. Play with color schemes and square arrangements to create everything from vintage-inspired Afghans to modern geometric designs.

- Bags and Totes: Join squares in specific patterns to create stylish handbags, purses, and totes. Add a fabric lining for durability and a professional finish.

- Garments: Yes, granny squares can even turn into wearable art. Whether a summery top assembled from floral-inspired squares or a whimsical scarf pieced together from vibrant hues, these squares offer a unique approach to crochet fashion.

The key is to view each square as a building block, a piece of a larger puzzle. You can assemble these blocks into functional and beautiful creations with patience and creativity.

Troubleshooting Tips

While working with granny squares can be immensely rewarding, it's challenging. Here are a few tips to keep your squares looking sharp and your projects progressing smoothly:

- Prevent Twisting: Ensure your squares lay flat by blocking them. Pin each square to a blocking board and lightly mist it with water, allowing it to dry into the correct shape. This step is crucial for maintaining uniformity, especially in larger projects.

- Maintain Tension: Consistent yarn tension is vital for uniform squares. If your squares vary in size, take a moment to assess your grip and tension. Practice on a few squares until you find a consistent rhythm.

- Count Your Stitches: Accuracy in stitch counts is essential for squares that align perfectly. Double-check your stitch count at the end of each round to avoid discrepancies that could throw off your project.

Embracing the classic granny square opens the door to a world of crochet rich with potential. These simple squares can be the foundation for projects as grand and diverse as your imagination allows. With each square, you build your skill and weave a piece of yourself into your creations, crafting items that carry the warmth of handmade charm.

7.5 Crochet a Diamond Popcorn Scarf: Your First Wearable Project

Crafting a scarf marks an exciting turn in your crochet adventure. It's the moment your creations step out into the world, not just as beautiful objects to admire but as functional pieces to wear and cherish. The right combination of yarn weight and hook size, a dash of basic stitch magic, and the final touches like blocking and customization transform simple yarn into a fashion statement.

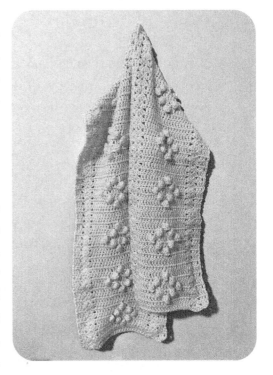

Yarn Weight and Hook Size Selection

Selecting the perfect yarn weight and corresponding hook size is like choosing the right ingredients for a recipe. The outcome significantly influences the scarf's texture, drape, and warmth. Lighter yarns, such as sport or DK, paired with a slightly larger hook, create a fabric with a gentle flow, ideal for transitional weather scarves. On the colder end, bulky yarns worked with hooks large enough to give the stitches room to breathe, resulting in cozy, warm scarves perfect for the heart of winter. This careful selection ensures your scarf looks the part and serves its purpose admirably.

Materials:

- Acrylic or bamboo worsted weight yarn #4(medium), approx. 500-800 yards, depending on desired length and thickness.

- Size H-8 (5 mm) crochet hook

- Scissors

- Yarn needle (for weaving in ends)

Abbreviations Used:

ch = chain

sc = single crochet

yo = yarn over

pc = popcorn stitch

rev pc = reverse popcorn

sk = skip

sts = stitches

Completed measurements 52 1/2 in. x 8 3/4 in.

Before crocheting the Diamond Popcorn Scarf, it is important to be comfortable with the popcorn and shell stitches as they are used in this pattern.

Popcorn stitch (pc) variations are used throughout the pattern and are described below:

- For right side Popcorn: 5 dc in next dc, pull up loop on hook to make it a bit loose, remove hook from loop, insert hook in top of first dc of this 5 dc group, put dropped loop back on hook and draw it through st on hook, tighten loop on hook, ch1, popcorn stitch (pc) made.

- For wrong side Reverse Popcorn: For the popcorn to puff out on the right side of scarf, after you have taken loop of hook, insert hook from back to front of the first dc of pc group, put dropped loop back on hook and draw it through loop on hook as before, tighten loop on hook, ch 1.

Diamond Popcorn Scarf Pattern

Row 1: Ch 36, sc in 2nd ch from hook. sc in each ch across. (35 sts). Turn

Row 2: (right side) ch 3, (counts as 1st dc for this row and rest of pattern), dc in each of next 2 sc, (sk 2 sc, 5 dc in next sc, sk next 2 sc, shell made), dc in next 19 sc, (sk 2 sc, 5 dc in next sc, sk 2 sc, shell made) dc in each of next 3 sc. Turn

Row 3: (wrong side) Repeat row 2

Row 4: (right side) ch 3, dc in each of next 2 dc, make shell (sk 2 dc, 5 dc in next dc, sk 2 dc), dc in next 9 dc, (5 dc in next dc, pull up loop on hook to make it a bit loose, remove hook from loop, insert hook in top of first dc of this 5 dc group, put dropped loop back on hook and draw it through st on hook, tight loop on hook, ch 1, popcorn (pc) made. dc in next 9 dc, make shell (sk 2 dc, 5 dc in next dc, sk 2 dc), dc in next 3 dc. Turn

Row 5: (wrong side) ch 3, dc in next 2 sts, make shell (sk 2 dc, 5 dc in next dc, sk 2 dc) dc in next 7 dc, 5 dc in next dc, pull up loop on hook to make it a bit lose, remove hook from loop, this time insert hook from the back to front of the top first dc st of the group, put dropped loop back on hook and draw it through st on hook as before, tighten loop on hook, ch 1, rev pc made. dc in next 3 dc, rev pc in next dc. 7 dc in next 7 dc, make shell (sk 2 dc, 5 dc in next dc, sk 2 dc) dc in next 3 dc. Turn

Row 6: (right side) ch 3, dc in next 2 sts, make shell (sk 2 sts, shell in next dc, sk next 2 dc), dc in next 5 dc, pc in next dc, dc in next 7 dc, pc in next dc. dc in next 5 dc, make shell in 3rd dc, dc in last 3 dc of row. Turn

Row 7: (wrong side) Repeat row 5

Row 8: (right side) Repeat row 4

Rows 9-11: Repeat row 2

Repeat Rows 4-11, 10 times

Repeat Rows 4-8 once more

Repeat Row 2 twice

Finish off.

Tips:

- Consistency is key. Maintain consistent tension throughout your work to ensure even stitches and edges.

- Take breaks to avoid hand strain, especially if you're working on your scarf for extended periods.

Scarf Variations

Once you've mastered the essential scarf, why stop there? The beauty of crochet lies in its versatility and the ease with which you can tweak a simple project to reflect your personal style. Consider these variations to infuse your scarf with a bit of flair:

- Adjusting Width and Length: Want a slimmer, more delicate scarf? Reduce the number of starting chains. Add more for a bold, statement piece. Length is just as easily adjusted; add rows until it wraps around you comfortably.

- Adding Fringes: Fringes offer a playful touch to the ends of your scarf. Cut lengths of yarn twice as long as you want the fringe to be, fold them in half, and use your hook to pull the looped end through the scarf's edge, then thread the loose ends through the loop and tighten. It's a fun, easy way to add movement and interest.

- Incorporating Stripes: Stripes are a fantastic way to play with color without changing the stitch pattern. Alternate your yarn colors every few rows for a vibrant effect, or add a single contrasting stripe for a pop of color.

With these simple ideas, your scarf can transform from an essential accessory into a bespoke piece that showcases your newfound skills and creative vision. It becomes more than just a way to keep warm; it's a symbol of your journey, a piece of wearable art that carries your unique touch.

7.6 Colorful Seasons: Crafting Your Year in a Crochet Temperature Blanket

A crochet temperature blanket is a creative project that captures the daily temperature of a specific location over a designated period, usually a year. The concept involves choosing a variety of yarn colors, each assigned to a particular temperature bracket. As you crochet, you use the color corresponding to your chosen location's daily high, low, or average temperature.

Meaning and Purpose:

The temperature blanket serves as a tangible diary or visual journal, representing the fluctuating climate patterns through the crochet lens. It's a unique way to document a year in your life, marking significant temperature-related events, seasons, and personal milestones. The blanket can symbolize the passage of time and changes in the environment or celebrate a specific year with personal significance, such as a birth year, a wedding, or a year of travel. Each blanket tells a unique story, reflecting the interplay between nature's rhythms and the crafter's dedication. Enjoy watching your blanket grow as the year progresses!

Special Thanks to Lisa Standish for the image of her beautiful Temperature Blanket

Materials:

- Cotton or acrylic worsted weight #4 (medium) yarns in various colors for temperature ranges

- Size H-8 (5mm) crochet hook

- Scissors

- Yarn needle (for weaving in ends)

Abbreviations Used:

ch = chain

sc = single crochet

dc = double crochet

sk = skip

st(s) = stitch (es)

* = repeat whatever follows the * as indicated

Temperature Blanket Crochet Pattern

Planning Phase:

1. Select Time Frame: Determine the period for your blanket, typically one year.

2. Research Temperatures: Obtain historical temperature data for your chosen location and time frame.

3. Yarn Color Selection: Assign specific yarn colors to represent different temperature ranges, such as every 10°F or °C increment.

4. Design Blanket Layout: To establish the size and structure of your blanket, decide whether each row or square will represent a day, week, etc.

Crochet Instructions:

Start: Begin with a slip knot on your hook.

Foundation Row: Chain (ch) the required number of stitches to achieve the desired width for your blanket, according to your selected stitch pattern.

Row 1: Select a stitch for your project, such as single crochet (sc), double crochet (dc) or moss stitch (pictured above). I've included moss stitch directions below. Crochet the first row using the yarn color that matches the temperature of your starting period.

Subsequent Rows: For each following day (or chosen time period), add a row in the yarn color that corresponds with that period's temperature. Ensure to:

- If using sc: Insert hook into the stitch, yarn over (yo), pull up a loop, yo again, and pull through both loops on the hook.

- If using dc: Yo, insert hook into stitch, yo, pull up a loop, yo, pull through two loops, yo again, pull through remaining two loops on hook.

Repeat: Continue adding rows for each day of your chosen time frame, changing yarn colors as necessary to reflect the temperature changes

If using moss stitch (AKA linen stitch, granite stitch, or woven stitch), you'll use sc and ch stitches below:

- Ch and even number of st(s) to achieve desired width of your blanket.

- Row 1: Sc in 4th ch from hook, * ch 1, sk 1 ch, sc in next ch, repeat from * across row. The last stitch will be a sc in the last ch.

- Row 2: Ch 2, turn. Sc in the next ch-1 sp from previous row, * ch 1, sk 1 sc, sc in next ch-1 space, repeat from * across row. The last stitch will be a sc worked into the space between the ch-2 turning ch and the sc from the prior row.

- Repeat row 2 until your blanket is as long as you'd like, adding rows for each day of your chosen time frame, changing colors as necessary to reflect the temperature changes.

Temperature Tracking:

- Maintain a Daily Log: Keep a record of daily temperatures using your preferred method.

- Regular Crochet Schedule: Dedicate time each day or week to crocheting the corresponding rows to keep up with your blanket's progress.

Finishing Touches:

Complete Final Row: Once you reach the end of your time frame, complete the last row following the established pattern.

Weave in Ends: Use a yarn needle to weave in all loose ends for a neat finish.

Optional Border: Add a single crochet border around the blanket for a polished edge. Start in any corner, ch 1 (counts as the first sc), and make sc evenly around the blanket, with 3 sc in each corner. Join with a slip stitch to the first sc and fasten off.

Tips:

- For color changes, fasten off and join new colors as needed.

- Adjust the blanket size by altering the number of chains in the foundation row or by modifying the chosen stitch pattern.

- For added personalization, consider using a different stitch or color to mark the start of each month or special dates.

- Consistency in stitch tension is crucial for a uniform look.

- Consider a spreadsheet for temperature tracking for easy reference.

- Starting and Ending Dates: While many choose to start on January 1st, you can begin a temperature blanket on any significant date.

- Adjust for Leap Year: If your project includes February 29th, decide how to incorporate this extra day.

- Temperature Fluctuations: If you live in an area with minor temperature variations, use a narrower range of temperatures for each color to ensure you use all your chosen colors and have more color change.

As we wrap up this exploration into the foundational projects for beginners, it's clear that each stitch and row brings you closer to turning yarn into something extraordinary. The world of crochet is full of possibilities, ranging from simple square coasters to practical washcloths, self-care bath poufs, versatile granny squares, and personal statement scarfs. Moreover, the journey of creating a temperature blanket is nothing short of fulfilling. These are some of the projects that can help you build a strong foundation for a satisfying crochet practice. They teach patience, precision, and the joy of creating something with your hands, skills you'll carry forward into more complex endeavors.

Chapter 8

The Calming Craft

CROCHET FOR MINDFULNESS AND RELAXATION

I n the quiet moments just before dawn, when the world is still asleep, and the first light makes its presence felt, a unique form of magic happens with a hook, some yarn, and your own two hands. Crochet transforms from a hobby into a soothing rhythm in these tranquil periods, a gentle dance of loops and knots that quiet the mind and comfort the soul. Here, in the soft embrace of the morning, we find crochet to be more than crafting; it's a pathway to peace, a method to unwind the knots in our minds as we tie knots in our yarn.

8.1 The Zen of Crochet: How Repetitive Motion Aids Relaxation

Soothing Rhythms

Picture this: the steady, gentle clicking of the crochet hook, the yarn smoothly gliding through your fingers, each stitch following the other in a comforting, predictable pattern. This repetition, much like the rhythmic sound of ocean waves or the steady beat of a heart, lulls the mind into a state of calm. Scientists have found that repetitive motions activate the body's relaxation response, counteracting the fight-or-flight stress response that many live with daily. This biological shift lowers blood pressure, reduces heart rate, and eases muscle tension, offering a physical sense of peace.

Focus and Flow

When you're deeply engaged in crocheting that challenging pattern or working on a piece that requires all your attention, the rest of the world fades away. This singular focus ushers you into what psychologists call 'flow' - a complete immersion in an activity. In flow, deadlines, personal worries, and even the passage of time seem to disappear. It's you and the project, nothing else. This mental state provides a break from stress and enhances happiness and satisfaction. It's a mental workout, flexing your concentration and problem-solving skills, leaving you refreshed and ready for whatever comes next.

Neurological Benefits

The benefits of engaging in crochet go deeper than just a feeling of relaxation. Neuroscientists have discovered that crafts like crochet can create new neural pathways, potentially fending off cognitive decline as we age. The focus required to follow a pattern or count stitches increases neural connectivity, keeping the brain agile and sharp. Additionally, the completion of a crochet project releases dopamine, a neurotransmitter associated with pleasure and reward, providing a natural mood boost.

Personal Anecdotes

Across the globe, countless individuals turn to crochet as a source of solace and joy. From those recovering from illness, finding strength and purpose in the stitches, to busy professionals who crochet during their commute to decompress before and after a hectic day. There are stories of people who have managed chronic pain through crochet, as the activity provided a distraction and a way to regain control over their body's narrative. These personal accounts underscore crochet's power as a tool for healing, demonstrating that behind every stitch, there's a story of resilience, recovery, and relaxation.

In this modern world, where the pace of life seems to accelerate with each passing day, finding moments of calm and mindfulness is crucial. Crochet offers a simple yet profound way to slow down and reconnect with ourselves in the quiet space between each stitch. It's a reminder that sometimes, the most effective form of self-care is found not in grand gestures but in the gentle rhythm of a crochet hook and yarn, moving together in harmony.

8.2 Setting Up a Mindful Crocheting Space

Crafting an area dedicated to your crochet endeavors does more than organize your supplies; it creates a sanctuary for your mind. This space becomes a cocoon, sheltering you from the whirlwind of daily life and allowing you to sink deeply into the meditative act of crocheting. Here's how you can curate this special nook. In this place, every element sings harmoniously to tranquility and mindfulness.

Creating a Calming Environment

- Simplicity is Key: Start with a clean, uncluttered area. A minimalist setup helps clear the mind, making slipping into a state of focused relaxation easier. Consider a comfortable chair by a window where natural light can spill over your work, enhancing the vibrant colors of your yarn.

- Nature's Touch: Incorporate elements of nature into your space. A potted plant or a vase of fresh flowers can breathe life into your surroundings, connecting you to the earth and its calming influence.

- Personal Zen Garden: Before you begin your crochet session, arrange a small area within your space that serves as a visual focal point for meditation. It could be a miniature Zen garden, a collection of smooth pebbles, or a simple water feature.

Minimizing Distractions

- Digital Detox: Make a conscious decision to reduce electronic interference. Turning off or muting notifications on your phone creates a buffer against the outside world, safeguarding your mindfulness zone.

- Time Block: Dedicate specific times for your crochet practice, informing household members, if necessary, to ensure this time remains uninterrupted. This isn't just about finding quiet time; it's about honoring your commitment to mindfulness and self-care.

- Organized Chaos: Keep your crocheting supplies neatly organized and within easy reach. A tidy workspace can prevent frustration and preserve the peaceful flow of your session. Consider using decorative baskets or containers that complement your space's aesthetic while keeping your yarn and tools orderly.

Incorporating Other Senses

- A Symphony of Scents: Aromatherapy can play a significant role in crafting a mindful environment. Lavender, known for its relaxing properties, or jasmine, with its uplifting scent, can be introduced through candles, diffusers, or essential oils. The right fragrance can anchor your mindfulness practice, signaling to your brain that it's time to unwind.

- The Soundtrack of Serenity: Background sounds can distract or deepen your crochet experience. Experiment with various audio backgrounds, such as soft instrumental music, nature sounds, or white noise. The gentle hum of a fan or a distant waterfall can provide an auditory backdrop that enhances concentration and relaxation.

- Lighting the Way: The quality of light in your crocheting space affects your ability to see your work and your overall mood. Natural light is ideal, but consider using soft, warm lighting as the day fades. Avoid harsh, fluorescent lights, opting for adjustable lamps that mimic the sun's gentle glow. This lighting reduces eye strain and creates an ambiance conducive to calm and focus.

Your crochet space reflects your inner world, a physical manifestation of your desire for peace and mindfulness. By thoughtfully selecting each element, from the yarn that slips through your fingers to the light that caresses your work, you craft more than just stunning pieces; you weave together moments of tranquility, stitch by loving stitch.

8.3 The Psychological Benefits of Completing a Project

When the final knot is tied and the last end is woven in, a moment of pure, unadulterated joy sweeps over a crocheter. This sensation, this peak of happiness at seeing a project come to fruition, is more than pride in a job well done. It's a complex mix of psychological rewards that feed into our sense of self, creativity, connections with others, and overall well-being.

Sense of Accomplishment

Finishing a crochet project can significantly boost one's self-esteem. It's the feeling you get when you look at your creation and think, "I made that." This sense of accomplishment is rooted in our psyche, reinforcing our belief in our abilities and skills. Every completed project, regardless of size, is a tangible reminder of our capability, creativity, and resilience. It's a powerful remedy to self-doubt, reinforcing our confidence in crafting skills and our capacity to set and achieve goals.

Creativity and Problem-Solving

Crochet does more than create beautiful items; it uniquely flexes the brain. Each project is a puzzle, a series of problems to be solved. How do you adapt a pattern to fit a particular size? What's the best way to incorporate a new stitch? These challenges require creative thinking and flexibility, pushing the brain to find new solutions. This cognitive workout boosts problem-solving skills, making them more readily available in other areas of life. Moreover, creating something new and bringing an idea to life through yarn and hook profoundly expresses creativity. It's a process that feeds the soul, offering a deep sense of satisfaction and fulfillment.

Social Connections

Completing a crochet project marks the beginning of its journey from maker to recipient. Whether it's a gift for a loved one, a donation to a charity, or a piece sold at a craft fair, each completed item has the potential to strengthen social bonds. These connections are vital to our psychological health, providing a sense of belonging and community. Gifting a crocheted item carries a piece of the maker's heart, a tangible expression of care and connection. Additionally, sharing projects online opens up a global community of like-minded individuals, offering support, inspiration, and camaraderie. This digital age has transformed crochet from a solitary activity into a shared experience, enriching lives across the globe.

Long-Term Well-being

Engaging regularly in crafts like crochet has been shown to have long-term benefits for mental health. Studies suggest that the repetitive motion and focused attention required can act as a form of meditation, reducing anxiety and depression. The sense of accomplishment and the strengthening of social connections contribute to a positive self-image and a feeling of belonging. Over time, these factors enhance overall well-being, making crafts valuable in maintaining mental health. Moreover, the cognitive challenge of learning new patterns and techniques can keep the mind sharp, offering a protective effect against cognitive decline.

In the world of crochet, each stitch is a step toward greater psychological well-being. The creation process, from the first loop to the last cut of the yarn, offers more than just a way to pass the time. It's a journey through creativity, challenge, connection, and achievement that enriches the crafter's life in countless ways.

With each completed project, crocheters weave a tapestry of experiences contributing to their personal growth, well-being, and sense of connection to the world around them.

As we wrap up this exploration into crochet as a form of mindfulness and mental health practice, let's carry forward the lessons learned. The stitches we create are not just part of a physical item but are interwoven with our mental and emotional fabric, contributing to our sense of self and connection to others. Crochet offers a unique blend of creativity, achievement, problem-solving, and social engagement, crucial to our happiness and life satisfaction.

Chapter 9

Smooth Stitches, No Glitches

*** Please scan the QR code to view the projects and images in color ***

I magine you're in the middle of baking a cake. You've mixed your batter; it's smooth and smells heavenly, and you're just about to pour it into the pan when you realize you forgot to preheat the oven. A minor hiccup, sure, but now you're on a slight detour, waiting for the oven to beep. In crochet, just like in baking, it's the little things that can throw a wrench in your plans. But fear not; for every missed stitch or uneven row, there's a solution, a way to keep your project on track without having to start from scratch. In this chapter, we'll tackle those common crochet hiccups head-on, ensuring your projects stay as smooth as your cake batter, even if the oven wasn't preheated on time.

Stitch Count Errors

Keeping your stitch count accurate is like ensuring you have the right ingredients for your recipe. If you're off, you might end up with a too-dense cake or a scarf that's unintentionally a shawl. Here's how to keep your stitches in check:

- Markers are Your Friends: Place stitch markers at the start and end of each row or round and at any critical points in between. Moving these markers as you progress makes it easier to spot if you've added or dropped a stitch.

- Frequent Counts: Regularly pause and count your stitches. It might seem tedious, especially if you're in the flow, but catching an error is like noticing you've added too much sugar before your cake goes into the oven - it's easier to fix.

- Visual Checks: Pay attention to the shape of your project. If it's starting to fan out or taper in, it's a visual cue that your stitch count might be off.

Incorrect Yarn Over

Yarn overs can be the secret ingredient that gives your project texture and depth. Still, they can lead to holes or overly loose stitches when done incorrectly. Perfecting your yarn over is similar to mastering the art of folding flour into your batter - it must be just right.

- Slow Down: Take your time with each yarn. Rushing can cause you to wrap the yarn too loosely or miss the hook altogether.

- Consistent Tension: Maintain a steady tension on your yarn. It should flow freely but not be so loose that it doesn't form a neat loop on your hook.

- Practice with Purpose: Set aside time to practice doing yarnovers and pulling through loops on a practice swatch. Repetition builds muscle memory, ensuring consistency in each yarn over.

Skipping Stitches

Skipping stitches can leave unwanted gaps in your project, like forgetting to add baking powder, leaving your cake flat and dense. To avoid this:

- Use a Guide: Mark each stitch in the instructions with a highlighter or pencil when working on a new pattern. This visual guide can help you stay on track.

- Touch, Don't Just Look: Sometimes, seeing where your next stitch should go is hard, especially in more textured patterns. Feel for the next stitch with your hook and fingers.

- Bright Lights and Magnifiers: Working in a well-lit area or using a magnifying glass can help you see each stitch clearly, ensuring none are missed.

Joining Rounds Correctly

Joining rounds is the cherry on top of any in-the-round project. A misstep here can lead to a jog or gap, disrupting the smooth finish of your work.

- Slip Stitch to Join: When joining rounds, a slip stitch into the first stitch of the round creates a smooth and less noticeable join.

- Invisible Join Technique: The invisible join technique can be a game-changer for projects where even the slightest jog is too much. Cut the yarn and pull it through the last stitch. Then, using a yarn needle, weave the end through the two loops of the first stitch of the round and back into the previous stitch, creating a seamless join.

- Continuous Rounds: For projects where a spiral finish is acceptable, working in continuous rounds without joining each round can eliminate any concern about jogs or gaps.

By addressing these common crochet mistakes head-on, you ensure your projects remain on course, beautiful, and as intended. Remember, every crocheter, no matter how experienced, encounters these hiccups. It's not the mistakes that define your work but how you adapt and overcome them. With these tips and tricks up your sleeve, you're well-equipped to tackle any project confidently, turning potential frustrations into opportunities for learning and growth.

9.1 The Art of Frogging: When and How to Undo Your Work

Realizing you need to undo your crochet work can feel like watching a cake fall in the oven after peeking through the glass too many times. It's deflating, to say the least. However, unraveling your crochet work can lead to a more polished final product, as a fallen cake can become the base for a delightful trifle. The trick lies in knowing when to pull the yarn and in doing so in a way that preserves both your materials and your spirit.

Recognizing the Need to Frog

There comes a point in many projects where a mistake is too big to ignore. The blanket may be skewing, or the hat wouldn't fit a melon, let alone a head. These are clear signs that a few rows back, something went awry. Spotting these issues can save you from a larger undo later. Regularly laying your work flat and measuring against the pattern's specifications can help you catch these discrepancies before they snowball.

Frogging Techniques

Undoing your work or 'frogging' need not be a hasty or harsh process. Here are steps to ensure you do it gently, preserving your yarn for a fresh start:

- Find a Starting Point: Identify the row or round where the error began. This is where you'll start unraveling.

- Slow and Steady: Gently pull the yarn, unraveling stitch by stitch. Rushing can cause knots and tangles, turning your yarn into a snarled mess.

- Roll as You Go: Wind the unraveled yarn into a loose ball. This keeps it from tangling and makes it easier to work with when you're ready to start again.

Saving Your Place

Before you start pulling at your stitches, securing your work is crucial. This way, you don't unravel more than necessary:

- Insert a Lifeline: Before unraveling, thread a piece of scrap yarn through the stitches of the row below your mistake. If you accidentally pull too far, this lifeline will stop the unraveling in its tracks.

- Use Stitch Markers: Place stitch markers on either side of the row where the mistake occurred. This visually marks where you need to work back to and helps keep the work organized as you unravel.

Emotional Resilience

Feeling disheartened by the need to undo your hard work is natural. Yet, every stitch you pull out is an opportunity to grow:

- Shift Your Perspective: Instead of seeing frogging as a step back, consider it a chance to refine your skills. Each redo is a lesson in patience and precision.

- Take Breaks: If the thought of unraveling hours of work is overwhelming, step away for a bit. A short break can dissipate frustration, allowing you to approach the task more clearly.

- Celebrate the Redo: When you start crocheting again, take a moment to appreciate the improved result. This positive reinforcement turns a potentially negative experience into a rewarding one.

Undoing your crochet work doesn't have to feel like a setback. With the right approach, it becomes part of the creative process, a testament to your commitment to quality and your resilience in the face of challenges.

9.2 Fixing Missed Stitches Without Starting Over

Discovering a missed stitch a few rows back can feel like finding a pebble in your shoe miles into a hike; it's small, but ignoring it might throw off your whole rhythm. Luckily, with cleverness and a couple of tricks up your sleeve, these little hiccups can mean something other than unraveling hours of work or accepting a less-than-perfect finish.

Identifying Missed Stitches

Spotting a missed stitch requires a keen eye and a bit of detective work. Here's how to catch them before they lead to more significant issues:

- Feel the Texture: Sometimes, your fingers catch what your eyes might miss. Gently running your hand over your work helps you detect inconsistencies in the texture that indicate a skipped stitch.

- Count Regularly: Make it a habit to count your stitches at the end of each section or color change. It's easier to track down where you might have gone astray when you have a recent "checkpoint."

- Look for Gaps: Visually scan your work for gaps or tightness in the fabric. Missed stitches often create a noticeable hole or cause the surrounding stitches to bunch up.

Ladder Correction Method

Once you've pinpointed where you missed a stitch, there's no need to pull out rows of work. The ladder correction method is your discreet fix-it tool:

- Secure the Run: Secure the loop directly above where the missed stitch should have been using a locking stitch marker. This prevents the work from unraveling further as you make your corrections.

- Ladder Up: With a crochet hook or a darning needle, gently pull up a loop from the row below through to the place of the missed stitch, mimicking the stitch you skipped. Continue pulling up loops through each successive row until you reach your current working row.

- Anchor the Correction: Work the newly created loop into your next stitch to secure it, or, if necessary, make a small knot and weave in the end discreetly.

Incorporating Fixes into the Design

Sometimes, despite our best efforts, a mistake becomes too integrated into the work to fix without notice. In these cases, creativity becomes your best friend:

- Turn Flaws into Features: Use the location of the missed stitch as an opportunity to add an embellishment or a design feature, such as a flower or a button, turning the mistake into a deliberate part of the pattern.

- Adjust the Pattern: If the missed stitch has caused a slight shift or gap, consider whether you can adjust the surrounding stitches to incorporate the error into the design by adding an increase or a decrease nearby to balance the tension.

Preventative Measures

The best way to deal with missed stitches is to prevent them from happening in the first place. Here are some strategies to keep your stitches on track:

- Use a Stitch Guide: A stitch guide or counter can be invaluable for patterns that require a large number of stitches. Markdown or click the counter each time you complete a stitch or set of stitches, as indicated in your pattern.

- Practice Mindful Crocheting: Sometimes, we miss stitches because our minds wander. Try to crochet in a quiet, distraction-free environment, especially when working on intricate patterns or learning a new technique.

- Choose the Right Tools: Ensure your lighting is adequate and your hooks are the correct size for your yarn. Poor visibility and mismatched tools can lead to missed stitches and uneven work.

- Take Breaks: Fatigue can lead to mistakes. Regular breaks help keep your mind fresh and your eyes sharp, reducing the likelihood of missing stitches.

Integrating these strategies into your crochet practice will reduce the frequency of missed stitches and enhance your work's overall quality and enjoyment. Remember, perfection in crochet, as in all crafts, is a journey, not a destination.

9.3 Troubleshooting Tension Issues for Even Stitches

When each stitch in your crochet project mirrors the next in size and shape, it's like watching a well-rehearsed orchestra - every note flows into the next in perfect harmony. However, achieving this level of uniformity in crochet often hinges on one critical factor: tension. Like the pressure of a bow on a violin string, the force you apply to your yarn as it glides through your fingers can make or break the melody of your stitches.

Understanding Tension

Tension in crochet isn't just about how tightly you're holding the yarn; it's the rhythm that guides the dance between your hook, your hands, and the yarn. It influences the fabric's drape, the stitch definition, and the overall dimensions of your project. Too tight, your fabric might curl and stiffen, refusing to lay flat. If it is too loose, you'll find a floppy, uneven texture lacking structure. The goal is to find that sweet spot where your stitches are consistent, creating a fabric that's as pleasing to the eye as it is to the touch.

Adjusting Your Grip

Finding comfort in your crochet grip is like getting to know a new dance partner. It takes time and a bit of experimentation. Here are a few ways to adjust your hold on the hook and yarn for better tension control:

- Hook Hold: Some crocheters prefer the pencil grip, holding their hook like a pencil for finer control, while others opt for the knife grip, with the hook resting in their palm. Try both to see which feels more natural and gives you better command over your stitches.

- Yarn Guide: How you feed the yarn through your fingers can significantly impact your tension. Looping the yarn once around your pinky finger before weaving it through your other fingers adds a touch of resistance that can help regulate the flow of yarn.

- Relaxed Shoulders and Elbows: Your arms affect how the yarn moves. Keep your shoulders down and your elbows at your side, creating a relaxed pathway for the yarn to travel from the skein to your hook.

Practicing Mindfulness

Crochet, at its core, is a mindful practice, a moment to breathe and focus on the movement in your hands. Paying attention to your body's cues can help you maintain even tension throughout your project:

- Notice Your Grip: Periodically check in with your hands. Are you gripping the hook or yarn too tightly? A light hold allows smoother stitches and reduces strain on your fingers and wrists.

- Breathe Deeply: It's easy to fall into shallow breathing when concentrating. Deep, even breaths can relax your muscles, loosening your grip and evening out your stitches.

- Take Breaks: Step away from your project every so often. Stretch your fingers, shake your hands, and return with a refreshed perspective and relaxed grip.

Tension Equalizers

Sometimes, despite our best efforts, maintaining consistent tension can be a challenge. Here are a few tools and techniques that can act as tension equalizers, helping keep your stitches uniform:

- Yarn Tension Devices: These small tools fit on your finger and provide a more consistent yarn flow, reducing tension variation.

- Yarn Bowls: Placing your yarn in a bowl helps control the speed at which it unravels, preventing it from either pooling at your feet or tugging back, which can disrupt your tension.

- Practice Yarn: Before starting on your project, work with a practice yarn similar in weight and texture to your project yarn. This warm-up lets you adjust your grip and tension without the pressure of the final piece.

In crochet, achieving even stitches is less about the destination and more about enjoying the journey. It's in the adjustments you make along the way, the awareness of your body's habits, and the tools you employ to bring harmony to your work. Through mindful practice and a willingness to explore different techniques, you'll find your tension sweet spot, where each stitch flows into the next, creating a beautiful piece to look at and a joy to make.

9.4 Repairing Finished Projects: Tips for Mending and Upcycling

When your cherished crochet item begins to show signs of wear or, heaven forbid, sustains damage, it's not the end of its story, far from it. With a needle, some yarn, and some creativity, you can breathe new life into your beloved pieces, ensuring they bring warmth and joy for years. Let's explore how to mend and upcycle, turning what might seem like setbacks into opportunities for rejuvenation and innovation.

Assessing the Damage

Before diving into repairs, take a moment to really look at your crochet item. Is it a small hole from a caught stitch, or are we talking about a larger area of wear? Understanding the extent of the damage is crucial for choosing the correct repair method. It's also an excellent time to decide whether a simple fix will do or if this is an opportunity to add a new element to the piece, enhancing its beauty and functionality.

Darning and Stitching

For holes and tears, darning is your go-to method. This process involves weaving yarn in and out of the damaged area, creating a fabric that fills the gap.

Here's how to approach it:

- Choose a yarn that matches the original work in color and weight. Opt for a contrasting shade for some flair if an exact match isn't available.

- Using a darning needle, weave in a grid pattern, first vertically, then horizontally, pulling gently to avoid puckering.

- Finish by weaving the ends into the surrounding stitches to secure your work.

This technique covers the damage and adds a decorative touch, especially when using contrasting or complementary colors.

Reinforcing Weak Areas

Areas that see a lot of wear, like the edges of a blanket or the underarms of a sweater, need reinforcing to prevent future damage. Crocheting an additional border or patching over these spots can provide extra durability. Consider using a slightly thicker yarn or a tighter stitch pattern for these reinforcements to ensure they stand up to the test of time.

Repurposing Projects

Sometimes, a project is beyond simple repairs, or its original form no longer serves your needs. That's when upcycling comes into play. Transform a frayed blanket into cozy pillow covers, or turn an outgrown sweater into a stylish tote bag. Here are a few ideas to get you started:

- Use segments of an old afghan to create a boho-chic wall hanging.

- Convert a shawl into a poncho with the addition of a simple seam.

- Stitch together worn dishcloths to create a unique, patchwork kitchen mat.

The possibilities are endless. With some imagination, items that might have been relegated to the back of the closet can find new purpose and add fresh zest to your home or wardrobe.

In this chapter, we've walked through the gentle art of mending and upcycling, transforming wear and tear into opportunities for creativity and renewal. From assessing the damage to making repairs, reinforcing weak spots, and giving old projects new life, we've covered the essentials of keeping your crochet items beautiful and functional.

Chapter 10

Embracing Crochet Creativity

EXPLORING COLOR CHOICES, MODIFICATIONS, AND JOURNALING

In every crocheter's journey, there comes a moment when the urge to break free from standard patterns becomes irresistible. It's similar to coloring outside the lines - a bit daring, perhaps, but oh, the excitement it brings! This chapter invites you to step off the beaten path, where you become your crochet canvas's artist and designer. Discover the thrill of selecting colors, making modifications, and documenting your unique journey through the pages of your crochet journal.

10.1 Customizing Projects with Color Choices and Modifications

Color Theory for Crocheters

Imagine your yarn stash as a vibrant garden, where each skein is a unique flower waiting to bloom into your next project. Understanding color theory is like knowing which flowers will create a stunning bouquet. It's not just about choosing colors you love; it's about how those colors interact on your crochet canvas.

- Harmonious Palettes: Start by picking a base color, then use a color wheel to find complementary shades. Similar colors (those next to each other on the wheel) blend beautifully for a serene vibe. Try contrasting colors from opposite sides of the wheel for some drama.

- Mood Setting: Colors evoke emotions. Soft blues and greens can create a calming effect, perfect for a cozy blanket. At the same time, vibrant reds and oranges energize a lively scarf.

- Experiment: Feel free to try unusual combinations on small swatches. Sometimes, the most striking palettes come from unexpected choices.

Adapting Patterns

Once you're armed with the perfect palette, it's time to make patterns work for you. Think of a pattern as a suggestion, not a command. Your creative flair can transform any design.

- Sizing Adjustments: If you're altering a wearable, remember that changing yarn or hook size affects the final dimensions. Adjust stitch counts proportionally to maintain the design's integrity while customizing the fit.

- Stitch Substitutions: Swap basic stitches with textured ones for a personal touch. A simple single crochet scarf becomes a tactile masterpiece with the addition of puff stitches or bobbles.

- Construction Changes: Play with construction methods. For instance, if a hat pattern starts from the top down, try working it from the bottom up. This might require recalculating increases and decreases but allows you to adjust the fit.

Making It Yours

Small changes can have a significant impact. These tiny tweaks make each project distinctly yours.

- Edging: Adding a unique border to a finished piece can drastically change its look. Lace edging can turn a simple shawl into an elegant wrap, while a fringe can add a bohemian flair to a blanket.

- Mix and Match: Combine elements from different patterns to create something new. For example, use the body of one sweater pattern with the sleeves of another or mix the motifs from various shawl designs.

- Personal Touches: Embellishments like buttons, beads, or embroidery can add depth and character. Even a matte versus a shiny button can change the garment's style.

Incorporating Personal Symbols

Your projects can tell your story through symbols and motifs that resonate with your life experiences, heritage, or dreams.

- Family Motifs: Incorporate symbols representing your family or heritage, such as Celtic knots for Irish roots or traditional motifs from your culture, into blanket squares.

- Nature Inspired: Draw inspiration from your favorite elements of nature. Leaves, flowers, waves, and animal motifs can all be part of your crochet designs, bringing the outdoors into your craft.

- Significant Numbers: Use stitch counts to embed personal numbers into your projects. For example, a scarf with a row repeating based on an important date or a pattern incorporating a loved one's favorite number adds meaning.

- Custom Graphghans: Graphghans use color changes to create pictures within crochet. Design a simple graph of a meaningful symbol or scene. This technique allows for endless creativity, transforming yarn into a personal narrative.

Incorporating these elements into your crochet makes each project unique. It embeds your creations with stories and meanings that transcend the stitches.

10.2 Documenting Your Crochet Journey: Keeping a Crochet Journal

Maintaining a crochet journal can be comparable to charting the course of a ship on the vast ocean of creativity. It's a tangible way to track progress, celebrate achievements, and reflect on the evolution of your skills and artistic vision. Recording your crochet adventures serves as a beacon, guiding you through the ebb and flow of inspiration and challenge and illuminating the path to mastery and self-discovery.

The Value of a Crochet Journal

A crochet journal acts as a repository for your creative endeavors, capturing the essence of each project from conception to completion. It's a place to celebrate victories, learn from stumbles, and observe growth over time. More than just a collection of notes, it reflects your journey, offering insights that can sharpen your skills and refine your artistic voice. This habit of documentation encourages mindfulness and intentionality in your craft, transforming each project into a chapter of your personal saga of stitches and yarn.

Chronicles to Keep

In the pages of your crochet journal, the story of each project unfolds. Here's what to capture:

- Project Details: Record each project's name, pattern source, and completion date. Note any modifications to the original design, ensuring you can replicate or adjust these changes in future works.

- Yarn Chronicles: Document the yarn used, including brand, color, weight, and required amount. This not only helps in recreating projects but also assists in stash management.

- Hooked on Hooks: Note the hook size and type for each project. Over time, you might prefer certain hooks with specific yarns or projects.

- Stitch by Stitch: For custom designs or modifications, jot down stitch counts, special techniques, and any challenges encountered. This technical log is invaluable for troubleshooting and innovation.

- Reflections and Revelations: Capture your thoughts and feelings about each project. What inspired it? How did it feel to complete it? What would you do differently next time?

A Palette of Memories

To elevate your journal from a simple logbook to a vibrant tapestry of your crochet life, consider these embellishments:

- Swatch Stories: Attach small swatches of yarn or mini versions of the project's pattern. These tactile memories add depth and color to your entries.

- Photographic Journey: Include photos of your projects, especially those given as gifts or sold. These snapshots capture the beauty and diversity of your work.

- Sketches and Dreams: Doodle designs, color combinations, or modifications. These visual notes can spark creativity and serve as the seeds for future projects.

- Patterns and Patches: Paste in snippets of patterns, especially for custom projects. This makes it easier to revisit and recreate favorite designs.

Threads of Connection

Sharing your crochet journal - or elements of it - with others weaves threads of connection through the fabric of the crochet community. Here's how:

- Online Show and Tell: Post photos of your journal pages, especially project snapshots and swatches, on social media or craft forums. This can inspire others and invite feedback and collaboration.

- Crochet Circles: Bring your journal to meetups. It can serve as a conversation starter and a way to share knowledge and tips with fellow enthusiasts.

- Gift Notes: When gifting a crocheted item, consider including a page from your journal detailing the project's backstory and specifics. This personal touch adds depth to the gift, making it even more special.

Incorporating these elements into your crocheting practice enriches not just your own experience but also that of the community around you. It turns individual projects into shared stories, lessons into collective wisdom, and personal growth into communal inspiration.

As we wrap up this exploration of documenting your crochet journey, remember that each entry, swatch, and reflection is a stitch in the broader canvas of your creative life. Your journal is more than just a record; it's a map of your journey, highlighting paths traveled and vistas yet to explore.

Keeping the Crochet Magic Alive

Now that you've mastered the basics and are on your way to becoming a crochet pro, it's time to pay it forward and share your newfound knowledge with others.

By leaving your honest review of this book on Amazon, you'll guide potential readers to the resources they need and ignite their passion for crochet.

Thank you for your invaluable contribution. Together, we can keep the art of crochet alive and thriving for generations to come.

Your biggest fan,
Ella Knotsley

Simply scan the QR code to leave your review:

1. Open your camera on your phone
2. Hover it over the QR code
3. Rate/review my book

Or visit this link to leave a review:
https://www.amazon.com/review/review-your-purchases/?asin=B0D73GHSPY

Conclusion

Wow, what a journey we've been on together, right? From that first moment, you picked up a crochet hook, feeling its weight and promise in your hand, to diving into the rich tapestry of yarns - each with its own story and texture. We've looped and stitched our way through the basics, danced around those decorative stitches that add sparkle to any piece, and found peace in the rhythm of our hooks. Crochet isn't just about making things; it's about creating moments, connections, and a space where everyone is welcome.

I hope you've felt the transformative power of crochet, how it's more than just yarn and stitches coming together. It's about crafting a little haven of calm in a busy world, building bridges in the crochet community, and discovering the sheer joy of creating something with your own two hands. Remember, this craft isn't about rushing to the finish line; it's about the journey, the yarns you'll meet along the way, and the stories you'll tell through your creations.

Suppose there's one piece of advice I'd love for you to carry with you. In that case, it's this: Be patient with yourself and cherish every stitch, even the ones you have to frog (remember, frogging is just a detour, not a defeat). Crochet, like any worthwhile skill, blossoms with time and practice. Embrace those learning moments, and let's not forget to laugh at our tangles and knots, for they're all part of our unique crochet tales.

I can't urge you enough to dive into the crochet community, whether online or in your neighborhood. The shared stories, the collective wisdom, and the warm embraces of fellow crafters can turn even the most daunting project into an adventure. And who knows? Your next CAL or charity project could introduce you to lifelong friends.

Let crochet be your mindful retreat. Let the hook and yarn be your meditation. There's something incredibly grounding about focusing on the here and now, stitch by stitch, breath by breath. And while you're at it, why not spread the joy? Teach someone to crochet, gift your creations, and watch those little acts of kindness ripple into the world.

Keep exploring, keep dreaming up projects, and start that crochet journal if you haven't already. It's a beautiful way to track your growth, celebrate your achievements, and sketch out all those dazzling ideas waiting to come to life.

From the bottom of my heart, thank you for joining me on this crochet journey. I hope these pages have inspired, comforted, and challenged you. I'm beyond grateful for the opportunity to share this craft with you, and I can't wait to see where your crochet path leads.

Here's to countless more stitches, projects, and shared moments. May your hooks be swift, your yarn be cozy, and your heart be full.

Happy crocheting,
Ella Knotsley

*** Please scan the QR code to view the projects and images in color ***

Acknowlededements

Special thanks to my family for their undying love and support.

Special thanks to Nancy Erickson for her amazing crochet skills, ideas, and assistance throughout creating my dream book.

Special thanks to Renate Kirkpatrick for the beautiful stitch illustrations - Ren's Fibre Art.

Special thanks to Crochet with Gabriella Rose for the beautiful Sunset Shore Blanket image.

Special thanks to Lisa Standish for the beautiful Temperature Blanket image

References

Ashlea. (2017, April 18). *Understanding Crochet Gauge and How to Measure It*. Heart Hook Home. https://hearthookhome.com/how-to-crochet-understanding-gauge-and-how-to-measure-gauge/

Ashlea. (2021, May 6). *3 Ways to Add Beads to Crochet*. Heart Hook Home. https://hearthookhome.com/3-ways-to-add-beads-to-crochet/

Benefits of knitting and crochet groups. (2023, June 12). KnitPal. https://knitpal.com/blogs/knitpal/benefits-of-knitting-and-crochet-groups#:~:text=From%20meeting%20like%2Dminded%20fiber%20artists%20and%20gaining%20inspiration%20and

Building Health Communities crochet classes have participants hooked. (2023, June 2). Www.sistersofcharityhealth.org. https://www.sistersofcharityhealth.org/blog/posts/building-health-communities-crochet-classes-have-participants-hooked/

Burns, P., & Van Der Meer, R. (2020). Happy Hookers: findings from an international study exploring the effects of crochet on wellbeing. *Perspectives in Public Health*, *141*(3), 175791392091196. https://doi.org/10.1177/1757913920911961

Cagle, K. (2022, September 23). *How To Get Perfect Crochet Tension*. Easy Crochet Patterns. https://easycrochet.com/how-to-get-perfect-tension-in-crochet/

Chan, T. (2023, May 23). *The 6 Mental Health Benefits of Knitting & Crocheting - Creativebug*. Creativebug - Craft Classes & Workshops - What Will You Make Today? https://blog.creativebug.com/the-mental-health-benefits-of-knitting-crocheting/

Coach, C. C. (2017, February 22). *I've reviewed 7 different crochet hooks so you don't have to!* Crochet Coach. https://crochetcoach.com/best-ergonomic-crochet-hooks/

Crochet Abbreviations and Definitions: 70 Must Know Terms. (n.d.). Darn Good Yarn. Retrieved March 5, 2024, from https://www.darngoodyarn.com/blogs/darn-good-blog/crochet-abbreviations-and-definitions-70-must-know-terms

Crochet Guild of America. (n.d.). Www.crochet.org. Retrieved April 6, 2024, from https://www.crochet.org/page/StartChapter

Curry, K. (2022, June 10). *Color Theory for Fiber Artist & Crafters*. Darn Good Yarn; Darn Good Yarn. https://www.darngoodyarn.com/blogs/darn-good-blog/color-theory-for-fiber-artists-and-crafters

Designing Your First Crochet Pattern - Beginner Tips. (2023, January 25). For the Frills. https://forthefrills.com/crochet-pattern-designing-for-beginners/

Diana. (2021, December 29). *Home - Adventures with Art*. Adventures with Art. https://adventureswithart.com/key-parts-of-a-crochet-hook/What

du Plessis, L. (n.d.). *How to Easily Upcycle Clothes with Crochet Techniques | Blog*. Domestika. Retrieved April 6, 2024, from https://www.domestika.org/en/blog/10541-how-to-easily-upcycle-clothes-with-crochet-techniques

EcoCult Staff. (2020, March 13). *The Best Sustainable and Ethical Knitting Yarns For Your Next Project*. Ecocult. https://ecocult.com/the-best-sustainable-and-ethical-knitting-yarns-for-your-next-project/

Farrow, K. (2022). Creating Purpose and Social Connection Through Crocheting and Knitting for People With Visual Impairments. *Journal of Visual Impairment & Blindness*, *116*(4), 574–578. https://doi.org/10.1177/0145482x221117180

Guide to Crochet Shell Stitch Variations with Patterns. (2023, June 4). Yarnspirations. https://www.yarnspirations.com/blogs/how-to/guide-to-crochet-shell-stitch-variations-with-patterns

Houtman, B. (2017, October 11). *How Crochet and Knitting Help the Brain*. Anxiety Resource Center. https://www.anxietyresourcecenter.org/2017/10/crochet-helps-brain/

How To Fix A Missed Stitch in Crochet (and Other Common Mistakes) - CrochetTalk. (2019, October 4). Crochettalk.com. https://crochettalk.com/fix-a-missed-stitch/

How to read crochet diagrams - DROPS Lessons / Pattern basics. (n.d.). Www.garnstudio.com. Retrieved March 5, 2024, from https://www.garnstudio.com/lesson.php?id=69&cid=17

Janice. (2023, November 1). *How to Fix Crochet Mistakes: 20 Errors and How to Correct Them*. Smart Knit Crocheting. https://www.smart-knit-crocheting.com/how-to-fix-crochet-mistakes.html

Joanne. (2024, February 5). *Crocheting the Left-Handed Way*. Love and Fibres. https://www.madewithloveandfibres.com/post/crocheting-the-left-handed-way

JOHANSON, M. (2022, September 14). *Learn How to Crochet the Popcorn Stitch*. The Spruce Crafts. https://www.thesprucecrafts.com/popcorn-crochet-stitch-tutorial-4688588

Kirkpatrick, R. (n.d.). *Stitch Overview*. Renate Kirkpatrick's Freeform Crochet~Knit~Fibre Designs. Retrieved April 6, 2024, from https://rensfibreart.com/crochet-tips-tricks-how-to-stitches/stitch-overview-how-to-read-patterns-symbols/

L, T. (2021, July 27). *Crochet Gauge: What Is It And Why It Matters*. TL Yarn Crafts. https://tlycblog.com/crochet-gauge-what-is-it-and-why-it-matters/

Lauren. (2012, December 10). *Bath Pouf Crochet Pattern*. Daisy Cottage Designs. https://daisycottagedesigns.net/bath-pouf-crochet-pattern/

Lindsey. (2023, June 1). *Natural vs. Synthetic Yarn - What You Need to Know*. Off the Beaten Hook. https://offthebeatenhook.com/natural-vs-synthetic-yarn/

Little, A. (2017, May 12). *What's the Right Crochet Hook for Beginners?* Craftsy | Www.craftsy.com. https://www.craftsy.com/post/crochet-hook-for-beginners/

Macaroni, S. (2023, February 25). *The BEST Yarn for Crochet Beginners: A COMPLETE Guide*. Sigoni Macaroni. https://www.sigonimacaroni.com/the-best-yarn-for-crochet-beginners/

O'Connor, A. M. (2021, January 27). *How To Create a Mindful Space*. Printique, an Adorama Company. https://www.printique.com/blog/how-to-create-mindful-calming-serene-space/

Rachel. (2022, June 5). *27 Advanced Crochet Stitches You Need to Try*. Desert Blossom Crafts. https://desertblossomcrafts.com/advanced-crochet-stitches/

RED HEART DESIGN TEAM. (2023, June 4). *Ultimate Guide to Left-Handed Crochet*. Yarnspirations. https://www.yarnspirations.com/blogs/how-to/ultimate-guide-to-left-handed-crochet#:~:text=In%20left%2Dhanded%20crochet%2C%20you

Rexroat, T. (2022, June 28). *Crochet Hook Materials: The Perfect Hook*. Interweave; Interweave. https://www.interweave.com/article/crochet/crochet-hook-materials-perfect-hook/

Rose, G. (2022, May 16). *Sunset Shore Baby Blanket Pattern*. Crochet with Gabriella Rose. https://www.crochetwithgabriellarose.com/sunset-shore-baby-blanket-pattern/

Says, M. (2014, October 30). *Crochet Spot» Blog Archive» Crochet Color Therapy - Crochet Patterns, Tutorials and News*. Crochetspot. https://www.crochetspot.com/crochet-color-therapy/

Staging a Knit-Out & Crochet Event | Welcome to the Craft Yarn Council. (n.d.). Www.craftyarncouncil.com. Retrieved April 6, 2024, from https://www.craftyarncouncil.com/knitoutbrochure.html

Stearns, S. (2021, June 19). *How to Crochet for Beginners*. Sarah Maker. https://sarahmaker.com/how-to-crochet/

Stearns, S. (2022, May 9). *How to Read Crochet Patterns for Beginners*. Sarah Maker. https://sarahmaker.com/read-crochet-pattern/

The Benefits of Knitting and Crocheting. (2022, March 17). Www.henryford.com. https://www.henryford.com/visitors/caregivers/care-connections/the-benefits-knitting-and-crochet

Tiffany. (2022, June 17). *Daisy Farm Crafts*. Daisy Farm Crafts. https://daisyfarmcrafts.com/10-organizations-to-donate-your-crochet/

tosner, sierra. (2018, June 6). *How To Make A Crochet Project Planner And Why You Need One*. Sweet Everly B. https://sweeteverlyb.com/crochet-project-planner/

Wilson, J. (2014). *This is your brain on crafting - CNN*. CNN. https://www.cnn.com/2014/03/25/health/brain-crafting-benefits/index.html

Yarn, Y. for. (2020, January 18). *Beginner's Guide to the Standard Yarn Weight System*. Yay for Yarn. https://yayforyarn.com/yarn-weights-guide/

Printed in Great Britain
by Amazon

47926220R00066